20/20
HINDSIGHT

IF I KNEW THEN WHAT I KNOW NOW I'D BE A WHOLE LOT RICHER

PARVIZ FIROUZGAR

20/20 Hindsight
If I knew then what I know now I'd be a lot richer

By
Parviz Firouzgar

Cover Design by Melodye Hunter
Copyright © 2015 by Parviz Firouzgar.
Interior Design by Zonoiko Arafat

ISBN: 978-0-9961446-9-8

Crescendo Publishing, LLC
300 Carlsbad Village Drive
Ste. 108A, #443
Carlsbad, California 92008-2999
www.CrescendoPublishing.com
GetPublished@CrescendoPublishing.com

Dedication

---•◦•---

This book is dedicated to those rare individuals willing to take risks, who get up one more time than they fall down.

I dedicate my work to those individuals who refuse to live in a sea of mediocrity, who never stop learning and who persist until they fulfill their dreams.

A Message from the Author

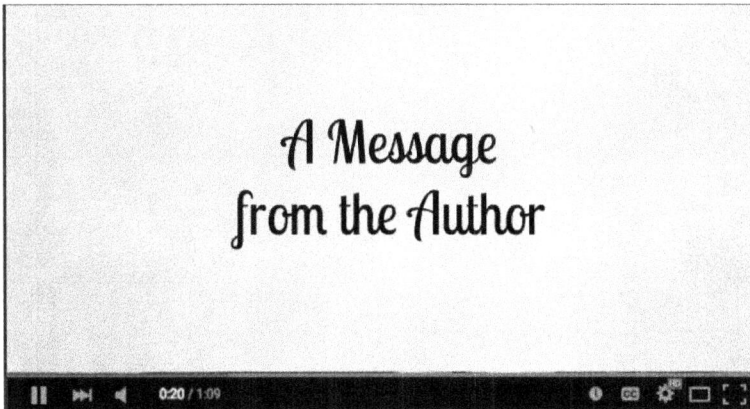

https://youtu.be/Rd5hZOVRUpg

Download a complimentary BONUS chapter from my new, forthcoming book, *"The Secrets of Wealth"* here:
http://www.parvizfirouzgar.com/

Table of Contents

Praise for 20/20 Hindsight

"I have known Parviz for better part of 30 years. His ability to land on his feet every time is nothing short of phenomenal. The essential ingredients that make him an unqualified success are laid out in this book. Read, implement, and profit from it."

Kayes Ahmed
President & CEO
Icelandic Design

"20/20 Hindsight is the business book every Chicken Soup, Rich Dad Poor Dad, The Secret, No Matter What, and Three Feet From GOLD, readers MUST read. Parviz, with his long time prestigious faculty participation at Forbes # 1 ranked entrepreneurial conference in the world - CEO SPACE - is the business leader everyone is seeking advice from. Buy ten and give them away to your best customers or family. They will all thank you - what a break through!"

Berny Dohrmann
Chairman
CEO Space International

"There is a big difference between book smarts and street smarts. Parviz provides the lessons you need to be street smart in your business."

Maria Crimi Speth
Intellectual Property Attorney
Jaburg Wilk

"They say the safest way to walk through the minefield is to walk in someone else's footsteps. If you don't see blood, keep going. Parviz lays out a step-by-step plan for success that not only keeps you out of harm's way but also provides a guide map to allow the success that is already inside you to shine through."

Ken Courtright
Author "Online Income: Navigating the Internet Minefield"

"In this day of entitlement thinking the pages of 20/20 Hindsight are a breath of fresh air. Do you want long-term success in business and life? Then let Parviz mentor you. Contained in these pages are the foundations of a truly fulfilled life, including the path to discovering our passion and true financial freedom."

Big Wave Dave / David James
DJ and On-Air Personality
95.9 AM KFSH (The FISH)

"This book is like reading a truly inspiring version of Sun Tzu's Art of War for entrepreneurs!"

B. Smith
Federal Regulator
Department of the Treasury

"20/20 Hindsight masterfully explains insightful shortcuts on the best practices of running and maintaining a successful business. 20/20 Hindsight may be the entrepreneur primer of the decade."

Stephen Smith
West Coast Sales and Compliance Manager
Soundcast Systems, Inc.

"If finding inspiration is like finding gold then Parviz Firouzgar is an alchemist who delivers a wealth of inspiration and how-to secrets for your success. Whether you have a small business, a big business or no business yet, do not miss this book!"

Tom Justin
Author
"How To Take No For An Answer And Still Succeed"

"Brilliant! It gets right to the point. Why should we make the mistakes that a successful businessman has already learned to avoid? Read this book and learn how YOU can avoid them. Thumbs up, way up!"

Suely Abboud
Founder
Tru Bru Organic Coffee

"20/20 Hindsight provides timeless advice that the beginning and experienced entrepreneur will benefit from greatly. This is a book you'll read more than once. I couldn't put it down. This is the advice I needed years ago. Parviz does an excellent job at illustrating his lessons with stories from his career as an entrepreneur."

Jill Lublin
3 Time Best Selling Author & International Speaker

"Success in business requires bold gestures but small moves, grand plans but step-by-step actions, strong team but individual accountability. Soak in every page of this book and you will be able to determine what to do, when to do it, and most importantly WHY! Let Parviz 'mentor' you through the pages of this book and you can't help but be successful."

Barry Spilchuk
Coauthor - A Cup of Chicken Soup for the Soul

Never underestimate the power of persistence.

"Never, never, never, give up!"

Introduction

It has been said that making your first million is the hardest. It's true. Your second million is a lot easier to earn than your first. Why? Because the second time around you know what you're doing. The path to your first million is paved with trial and error, wasted time, and expensive lessons. Thereafter it's a path you've already travelled and you know the way. You know where all the dead-end streets are, and you've learned to avoid them.

How would you like to learn how to avoid those dead-end streets from the very beginning by putting yourself on the right path from day one? Interested? If so, keep reading. That's what I'm about to teach you.

Consider this, if you take away everything a millionaire owns, he will typically make it all back almost every time. In fact, he'll make it all back in much less time than it took him to make his fortune the first time around. This is because he's no longer stabbing around blindly in the dark, trying to figure out how to get from A to B. You see, making money isn't that difficult … if you know how to do it. Any self-made millionaire will tell you that. What is hard is discovering the path from A to B if you've never travelled down that road before.

I used to tell people that I'm already working on my second million … I gave up on the first. That was obviously said in jest, but what if you could genuinely skip ahead to possessing that unique set of skills that comes with already having earned your first fortune? It would have made a huge difference for me. If I'd known then what I know now, I really would be a lot richer now.

With the right knowledge, *your* first million will come much easier and faster. That, in a nutshell, is the promise of this book. My 20/20 hindsight will be your 20/20 foresight.

After more than twenty-five years as an entrepreneur in a plethora of unrelated businesses, having achieved wealth and success, and having learned how to hold on to it, I now know that I could have achieved the same in a lot less time. The missing ingredient was a mentor or a book such as this one to give me some targeted advice early on. Learning it on my own through trial and error cost me a small fortune in expensive mistakes and took many extra years.

They say that when the student is ready, the teacher will appear. I was definitely ready. Unfortunately, for a long time experience was the only available teacher to teach me the lessons I needed to learn. Some lessons you'll also have to learn through experience as some lessons can only be learned that way. There's simply no substitute for experience. But not all lessons. Knowing certain "wisdoms" ahead of time will accelerate your learning process and save you time and money. For many, it will even mean the difference between success and failure.

Twenty-five years of business successes, and some business failures, have uniquely qualified me to be your mentor and save you years of costly mistakes. I made plenty of them, but with the lessons I'll share with you, you won't have to.

During my entrepreneurial business career, I've started almost a dozen different companies in a variety of unrelated fields. Sometimes I ran several companies at the same time. I've mailed millions of pieces of mail in a mail-order business. I've run sweepstakes promotions and written books, even a romance novel. I've written dozens of business plans for start-up ventures and helped many of these companies raise millions of dollars. I've worked in the charitable arena and supported in excess of 2,300 needy kids in underdeveloped countries after just one year of operations ... and I accomplished that by using a method of raising funds that had never been attempted before. I was a radio talk show host for two years and an instructor at business forums. I even had a mortgage company with over 500 loan officers. Most recently I've been in the precious metals and diamond business, including owning a gold mine.

My sincere desire is that this book becomes your gold mine.

My businesses typically involved a process that had never been attempted before or something I had never done before and that I had zero experience in. This has always been my unique formula, finding something that sounds exceptionally interesting and that I could be truly passionate about, but something that I knew nothing about. Each time I jumped in and learned as I went along. That will clearly not work for everyone, but it provided me with the motivation to get up every morning as I thrived on learning something new that intrigued me.

When I started out, if you had told me that in a few years I'd be an expert in sweepstakes promotions, I would have laughed. But it happened. If you had told me that I would soon learn to grade and price diamonds of any size and quality, I would have told you that you were crazy. But it also happened. Likewise with becoming a radio talk show host, inventing a new way of supporting needy children around the world, and owning a gold mine. The point is that nothing is out of our reach, for me or for you. If you want something bad enough and you're willing to go after it with the right combination of planning and persistence, nothing can stand in your way.

I see myself as being something of an inventor and innovator as I've had a few really great ideas, but that's actually nothing to brag about as it's not unusual. We've all had some great ideas. Ideas are a dime a dozen. However, although ideas are a dime a dozen, the people who turn them into reality are priceless. And that's the part you need to focus on — how to make your idea happen no matter what obstacles appear to be standing in your way. You can do it, I promise you. Use my formula by just getting out there and doing it.

Nike said it best, "Just Do It!" If you pay close attention to the lessons in this book, it will prepare you to get there sooner, cheaper, and without fail.

I guess you could call me a serial entrepreneur. I love to create something out of nothing, especially if it's something that's never been tried before. By nature I'm an inventor, not necessarily of new products but of new methods and means of accomplishing things. As I already mentioned, that in itself is not a big deal, but I turned my ideas into reality. Very few people can make that claim. Will you join me?

Each business I started was totally unrelated to the previous one. I just dove into whatever I was passionate about at the time with no regard to my total lack of experience in the field. Some of my ventures were truly groundbreaking. Even at twenty-two years of age, my first fledgling business was new and unproven, a delivery service for fast-food restaurants in Marina del Rey, California.

The restaurants I serviced did not deliver. We did it for them for a $3 delivery fee plus tips. Our customers would call us and have us to go to McDonald's or wherever and deliver whatever their appetite desired. I called the company Roadrunner, and I did this long before these types of delivery services became fashionable all over southern California. To the best of my knowledge, mine was the first.

Most of my businesses were successful, some of them smashingly so. I know the euphoria of seeing a pet project blossom into something incredible and profitable. It's an indescribable feeling when all your moves turn to gold and your bank accounts continue to grow. But I also learned that it doesn't always last. I know what it's like to have your whole world come crashing down around you without warning from one day to the next. One day you're king of the hill, and the next day your life is torn to shreds and you lose everything you own without warning. Short of losing a loved one, these are the deepest depths of despair imaginable.

Toward the end of this book, I'll share one of these experiences with you so that you can see how every setback can turn into something new and greater than what preceded it. I know what it's like to be on both sides of the aisle. I've been rich and I've been poor, and as entertainer Sophie Tucker once eloquently concluded, rich is better.

My failures taught me the most valuable lessons of all, much more valuable in fact than my successes. For this reason, today I'm more interested in people's failures than their successes because it's our failures that teach us the lessons we need to ensure that our next success lasts for the rest of our life. Our first success is often fleeting as we think we can do no wrong and our ego gets way out of control. Then it all comes crashing down because of the flawed character traits that surface and begin to sabotage what we worked so hard to build. It's our failures that positively mold our character, not our successes. For me, humility and gratitude are at the top of that list. I now value them beyond anything else.

They say that every wealthy person who has achieved *lasting* success has gone broke at least twice. Well, I'm the perfect example. I've gone from affluent to broke twice. Now I know what to do to ensure it'll never happen to me again, and I want to share what I've learned so that it doesn't ever happen to you either.

I once saw a photograph in a magazine of a tiny three-year-old boy bumping foreheads with a fully grown male lion. Only a few iron bars of the lion's cage separated them. The caption underneath read, "True character is revealed when you come face to face with adversity." That image has been imprinted on my mind ever since. Adversity was my teacher but adversity does not have to be your teacher. This book, containing the right information ahead of time, can be your teacher and guide.

I don't want to imply that successes are not worth learning from. Not at all. If you want to be a millionaire, you should hang out with millionaires. Learn from those who have done it before. Conversely, examine what poor people do and then stop doing those things.

Learning from successful people and successful businesses is a vital ingredient in your education. Who is better qualified to teach you than the person who has actually done it? It's ironic how we grow up doing the exact opposite. We seek advice from family, friends, and school guidance counselors, none of whom may have ever experienced wealth and success. How can we expect to learn the secrets of wealth from them? It's like asking a beginning ice skater how to become an Olympic gold medalist ice skater. Good luck.

Would you get advice on how to jump out of an airplane from 12,000 feet from someone who has never parachuted before? I hope not. I would only ask someone who has jumped at least 500 times and lived to tell about it. Likewise, don't ask an employee who makes $50,000 a year how to make a million dollars. They'll undoubtedly give you well-meaning advice, but chances are it will be worthless.

What I'm saying is that your advice should come from someone whose success is the result of real-world experience, from having been there and having done it, and preferably from someone who has also had periods of hardship to get there. Such advice is much better qualified than advice from someone who throws textbook theory at you, or just got lucky, or fell into wealth by inheritance or accident. This also applies when you evaluate an individual as a potential partner. You're much better off doing business with someone who has fallen down a few times and who has had to pull him or herself out of an abyss once or twice.

People who have never failed have been shortchanged by life. It causes them to think they can do no wrong. The sad reality is that our success will become the seed for our future failure. I know because it happened to me. It was failure that taught me the value of money, gratitude, and humility. Failure also taught me the value of knowing how much I have left to learn, all of which are infinitely more precious than money itself.

We succeed by making good judgments. Good judgments come from experience. Experience comes from making bad judgments. I want to reduce the number of bad judgments you'll make by sharing my experiences with you.

You'll still make some bad judgments, but don't let that deter you from moving forward. If the secret to success had to be distilled into a single piece of advice, it would be to get up one more time than you fall down. If you flip a coin often enough, eventually it will come up heads.

There's a difference between success and *lasting* success. Success can be experienced by almost anyone with a properly executed plan. But success is generally fleeting for those experiencing it for the first time. For *lasting* success and the most important lessons in life, failure is often the best teacher because people don't learn the really tough lessons voluntarily, nor do people change because they want to. People learn and change because they have to. And they have to because they just failed.

Bob Marley once said, "You never know how strong you are, until being strong is your only choice."

The problem with one's first success is that it often causes complacency, and complacency is death to business. Complacency causes a business to stop growing, changing, and innovating. It's doomed to fail. In business you can never stand still. A business that stands still is actually going backwards because there's someone out there innovating, thereby doing a better competitive job than you. They'll eventually overtake you, and you'll be left standing there wondering what happened. So if you're too busy enjoying your success, you may soon be wondering where it suddenly went.

Many of the lessons contained in the following pages are not taught in business school or anywhere else. You won't find them as part of any curriculum. They are the result of experience, not theory. However, it's possible to avoid having to learn many of these lessons through trial and error. It's possible to achieve lasting success without the periods of despair that are typically life's teacher. Again, I say this with a caveat. Some things cannot be taught; they must be learned through experience as I had to learn them. You can go through management training for years and still not know how to properly manage people until you learn by doing. One of my chapters will address that very issue.

In some areas there are no shortcuts. However, it's possible to shave off years of trial and error and tens or even hundreds of thousands of wasted dollars that pay for your mistakes in numerous other areas. That's what this book will do for you. Beyond the few important lessons you'll have to learn on your own, here are some you won't have to waste time and money over. I already did that for you.

By the way, if you're still somewhat inexperienced in business, it's possible that you'll think you're the exception to the rule as you go through this text. You may disagree with some of what I say and think that you can do it right the first time *and* keep it without losing it all. Here's where you'll just have to take a leap of faith by accepting that I'm talking about something outside your field of experience, but well within mine. Ironically, acknowledging your lack of experience may be outside your field of experience. Furthermore, with some people the problem may not be that they don't know what they don't know. Rather, the problem may be that what they think they know just isn't so. Hence I ask you to take this leap of faith. Trust me. You don't know what you don't know, and that which is unknown to you is simply not yet an ingredient in your reasoning.

Still not sure that I may be right? Consider this: Why is it that despite the vast technology and knowledge gap between young and old, where the latest college graduates have computer and technology skills vastly superior to those of the average middle-aged executive, virtually any genuinely successful company has seasoned managers at its helm and not twenty-somethings? The reason is experience. You can have a dozen advanced degrees in business management that took you a decade or more to achieve, yet none of them can substitute for real-life experience. Theory and technical knowhow are simply not the same thing as experience. Only individuals with experience truly understand this, and you can recognize them because they're the only ones who admit to a time when they were not yet ready to be boss. Their business "character" had not yet been developed although they may have had first-class technical skills. The inexperienced person, no matter how educated or intelligent, will oftentimes insist that they can do it better than the boss. Maybe a few can, but most cannot. They simply lack experience to properly guide, inspire, and manage other people.

I know this ... from what else? Experience. During my early twenties I temporarily entered the corporate world and worked for MCI Communications for six years. I was a highly successful salesperson with a burning desire to go into management. I knew I could do better than some of the middle managers I reported to. Their only priority appeared to be their own survival or advancement, not the customer, company, or its salespeople (who are key to generating the company's revenues). This made no sense to me, and I wanted to do better than they did. But no matter how hard I tried or how many times I applied for a promotion, I never moved into management. So I left MCI and followed my true calling, that of the entrepreneur. Of course today, with 20/20 hindsight, I know why I didn't get promoted. I wasn't ready to manage people, even if my imagined methods were better for the company's business than the actions of the managers I reported to. Today I know that there's a whole lot more to it than what you learn by reading the *One Minute Manager®*.

Some things just cannot be taught; you have to experience them yourself. But your learning curve can be vastly accelerated with the right knowledge up front. I once asked myself, "What if I knew then what I know now?" Simple, I'd be a lot richer and even more successful right now. I could have also spared myself some excruciating and emotionally devastating setbacks. Having a mentor at the right time with the right wisdom to share with me would have made the difference. Now, with 20/20 hindsight, I can be that mentor for you. I can save you years of trial and error, tens or even hundreds of thousands of wasted dollars. Maybe I can even spare you the depths of failure I had to experience to learn some of these lessons.

Many of the business lessons I'll share with you are also life lessons, inseparable from how you conduct yourself in everyday life. As you lead your life and learn from the mistakes you make, so will your business move in tandem.

I'll show you what the ingredients are to predictably create success, how to keep your successes from turning into failures, and thereby how to make your success last. You'll receive the benefit of my 20/20 hindsight. I'll illustrate many of the concepts by relating them to the businesses or projects where I applied or learned them. Some of these lessons have never appeared in any business book, at least any that I know of, and I've read hundreds.

Attaining and maintaining success results from foreknowledge and having a viable plan. To benefit from this book, it doesn't matter whether you're just starting out or if you're already running a business with millions of dollars in revenues. These are shortcuts that will accelerate your momentum regardless of your starting point.

Are you ready for hard work, perseverance, and applying the knowledge I'll share with you? Trust me when I tell you this: I never inherited a dime, but in the end I already had everything I needed to succeed — and so do you. I had a burning desire and a "failure is not an option" attitude. I intuitively knew that if the desire is strong enough, then the impossible becomes merely difficult.

Lucky? Yes, I was lucky. I learned that the harder I worked, the luckier I got. Did I have a privileged background? Yes, to a certain degree. I grew up in many different countries, which broadened my horizon, and I had a good family upbringing. But I also dropped out of college, and at the lowest point in my life, I ate out of a trash can in Hollywood because I had no money, and my family was on a different continent. From there my life could be summed up with a quote I hope you'll take to heart and apply for yourself: "There's only one way to predict the future and that is to create it." Now it's time for you to create your future using the lessons I'll teach you.

I once jokingly said that hindsight is like foresight, except there's no future in it. On the surface this sounds true, but in reality hindsight can be the foundation for a better future. This book is the result of looking back over my business career and identifying the many lessons I learned from my mistakes and from information I didn't have at the time. Thus my 20/20 hindsight can be the foundation for a better future for anyone who reads and applies this text.

Many of the passages in this text contain multiple important points, often concentrated into a small space. Hence this is not a text you want to skim over or speed-read. In fact, I suggest reading it more than once. Each time there should be new revelations that can help you accelerate your path to success. You may find points that you missed the first time, or you may make important connections with other passages in this text that cannot be made during the first reading.

"That some should be rich shows that others may become rich." – Abraham Lincoln

Lesson #1

Partnerships don't work ... unless you do this!

Partnerships don't work ... unless you do this!

Partnerships frequently fail because of the way most people go about them. In fact, the majority of partnerships are dead on arrival. So let's examine why many partnerships fail, and what needs to be done from the beginning to protect them.

The rationale for having a partner makes all the sense in the world. What better way to go into business than by sharing risks and expenses while having your partner contribute additional time and expertise to the venture? In theory that sounds great, but reality is not so kind.

Partnerships are a virtually guaranteed recipe for disaster within as little as a few short months because of the most unexpected and unlikely of reasons. Almost every would-be entrepreneur who has tried going into business with someone else has failed at it and wondered what happened while blaming it all on the other partner.

The truth is that partnerships fail because of the most surprising of foundations, good intentions. In fact, it's precisely what you believed to be your partnership's strength that ends up being its Achilles' heel. Good intentions end up replacing good business sense. Ironically it was Karl Marx who said that the road to hell is paved with good intentions, and he was right. Welcome to business hell!

Consider the typical scenario of going into business with a partner. You choose someone you deem similarly qualified as you, someone whom you know, like, and trust. You want to motivate them to work as hard as you, so you go into an equal partnership where everything gets shared equally: decisions, labor, risks, and rewards. You want your partner to feel that he or she is your equal, so there will be no boss at the partnership level. Equality rules, and you both share and show nothing but the most sincere good intentions. You feel that both your business futures and your friendship are secure because you know that neither of you has the authority to exert their will over the other person. What can possibly go wrong?

Precious few people have figured out why this formula is a recipe for business and personal disaster, and even fewer have managed to avoid its pitfalls the first time they enter into a partnership.

Years ago I started a small computer sales and service company with a friend. We sold PCs to individuals and small businesses and provided networking, education, and configuration services. My friend and partner was the computer expert, and I had more general business experience than he. This appeared to be a good combination and provided us with a clear division of labor. He had the technical mind, and I had the business mind. And we both had nothing but good intentions.

Our business barely lasted three months. We even ended up in court together. Our problems began over the silliest issue, the design of our logo. We decided that I would design it, but when I did, my partner didn't like it. In fact, he didn't hesitate to claim that he could do better. Obviously I had an issue with this because I actually had some real-life creative design experience. He did not. That's why I was assigned with the task in the first place. I knew what I was doing, and once completed, I was emotionally attached to my design.

Our disagreement eventually turned into hostility as our egos went to war. What we surely both agreed should have been an insignificant disagreement eventually spiraled out of control. This minor dispute literally killed the company.

So here are the ingredients that are at the root of failed partnerships: good intentions, human nature, and ego. The offer of equality comes from our good intentions to make the partnership work. Unfortunately, a partnership where everything is shared equally rarely works, but it's precisely these types of partnerships that everyone starts.

Consider that what eventually happens in an equal partnership is a pure expression of human nature. We all have an ego — part of it strong, part of it weak or fragile. A strong ego is a healthy ego. It's an expression of self-confidence. A fragile ego is at the root of self-indulgence where self-righteousness and a "know it all" and "I'm always right" attitude surface. Fragile egos cause business breakups, relationship breakups, and even wars between nations. We all have strong and fragile egos in different proportions. Whatever those proportions are, some part, no matter how small, is on the fragile side. This is the side of us that gets emotionally attached, offended, defensive, and self-righteous. Some live their entire lives in this state of egoism. We all eventually demonstrate the darker side of our humanity, even if some of us do so only to a small degree. And this is the part of us that makes an equal partnership a mathematical impossibility to operate as intended.

What typically happens is that two people determine that they would be great partners in a new business for any number of reasons. They get along great, never argue, and complement each other on experience and expertise. Neither partner, because of their good intentions, would dare suggest anything but equality. A simple partnership agreement may even be drawn up outlining how everything will be shared equally. The overriding focus in that agreement will be equality in decision making and equality in reaping the financial rewards. But it's precisely because of the well-crafted and well-intentioned equality clauses that the partnership will sink into oblivion.

The path toward destruction typically follows a common pattern. The business is started and everything is shared as equally as possible, especially decisions. The beginning of the partnership actually does work temporarily while many major decisions have to be made. The euphoria of having started a new business together makes disagreements almost unthinkable. Each partner respectfully involves the other person, and agreement on the major issues is overwhelmingly frequent.

Once the major decisions have been made, the time comes for some minor decisions, such as the design of a logo. Suddenly a disagreement pops up, and both sides will readily demonstrate emotional attachment to their viewpoint. This is ego, and it's human nature. The problem is that there's no tiebreaker. Who should give in? Who wins the disagreement? There's no third party to cast a deciding vote, and neither of the two partners have veto power. Sooner or later, one or more fragile egos are unveiled. The underlying issue soon becomes secondary as a minor disagreement turns into a major battle of egos. Even if the partnership remains operational for a while, overcoming several of these petty issues will sooner or later end with unfortunate results.

Business partnerships typically do not have the intimate emotional bonds that relationships have to fall back on. In fact, when money is at stake, the situation can become rapidly unstable because we want to protect our personal investment.

Equal partnerships are made worse when friends or family are involved. As they say, "The best thing about doing business with someone who knows you is that they know you. And the worst thing about doing business with someone who knows you is that they know you."

There are a couple ways to make a partnership work, but few will heed this advice until they have failed at least once and gained the wisdom of 20/20 hindsight. The most effective way is to create a partnership with multiple departments where each department has a leader. This means that no area of the business should be without a boss who has final authority.

Let's say there are two partners in a business that involves marketing, advertising, accounting, sales, and technical knowhow. Each discipline should be viewed as its own department, and each department needs a boss. Responsibilities should be roughly equal on both sides. Partner A may have the final say in the areas of advertising, marketing, and sales. Partner B may have the final say in accounting, finance, and the technical side of the business. This needs to be put in writing. Each partner should have undisputed veto power in each of their respective departments or areas of greater expertise as agreed upon at the beginning ... and clearly spelled out in a partnership agreement.

There's still plenty of room for good intentions and mutual respect. It can be agreed and practiced that all decisions will still be made with the involvement of the other partner. However, if there's an irreconcilable disagreement, then the partner with veto power in that particular field gets no resistance from the other side when enforcing his will. In that department he is boss. Now the partnership has a chance of working.

As mentioned previously, partnerships with friends and family are particularly fragile and hard to make work. Sadly, more often than not, the friendship is destroyed along with the company. That's why any kind of business deals that involve friends and family, not just partnerships, *must* be put into writing. They have to be treated in the same way as a business venture with someone who is a complete stranger to you. Only then is the friendship protected. Here is an example.

My best friend is Jim. Several years ago he married his fiancée Denise, and I was best man at their wedding. Unfortunately, Jim wasn't doing great financially at the time, and for some reasons beyond Jim's control, his credit was also less than stellar. Of course, Jim and Denise wanted what all newlyweds want, a home to call their own. I gently introduced a seed into our conversation, the possibility of me financing a home for them. I thought of a way to make it a win-win scenario, which incidentally is the only type of agreements that I make. My philosophy is that nobody should ever walk away feeling that he or she got the better end of the deal. I believe in karma, and therefore if you take advantage of someone, it will eventually come back to bite you.

Anyway, my idea was to buy my friends a home that they would rent from me for one year and then purchase from me at slightly less than fair market appreciation. One side saved a little while the other side made a little, win-win. Additionally, my friends had the opportunity for home ownership without actually being able to qualify for it at that time. And they would have a year's worth of rent payments essentially going toward equity. If, at the end of the first year, they weren't yet in a position to buy the home from me, they agreed to rent for an additional year with the right to purchase the home at any time on the same terms during that second year. If after the second year they still couldn't or didn't want to buy the home, my friends could walk away from it, and I'd be able to sell the home on the open market.

We fine-tuned the concept, and it all appeared to make sense. It was a go. And then we put it all in writing with every detail spelled out.

The end result was that my friends became happy homeowners for several years as they managed to buy the property from me after about a year and a half of rental occupancy. I made a modest profit on my investment, the down payment, and I was able to help my friends begin their new life together as homeowners. It worked out better than expected as the property appreciated beyond all our expectations, so Jim and Denise's equity position continued to grow. Throughout this transaction nothing was assumed, nothing was agreed upon without putting it in writing, and a win-win situation was thereby not left to chance or good intentions. Jim and I are still the best of friends.

In case you're one of those rare individuals who has a partnership that appears to be working or even thriving, consider yourself very fortunate. You're in the minority. As with anything there are exceptions. All the lessons in this book have exceptions.

Don't create partnerships based only on good intentions. Create win-win partnerships that have a chance of surviving. Business is business, even with friends and family. Put it in writing, and above all, make sure every aspect of the business has one of the partners with final authority when inevitable disagreements arise.

In my most recent business venture I have two partners. Our structure is a little different from the structure I just described. Our current structure requires a certain amount of maturity that comes only from years of experience, so it's not for everyone. Nonetheless, I'll describe it here because there are several similarities.

In our three-way partnership, without a doubt I have by far the most business experience. The business concept was my idea, and I would have pursued it with or without partners. I invited two friends to join me, and Jim was one of them. Because I knew that my business experience was vital to the success of the partnership and the business in general, I insisted that I have veto rights over all major decisions. My partners wisely agreed because they knew my track record. But here's what has made our partnership thrive beyond expectations over the past five years: In all those years I've used my veto power in only two or three instances. We still make all decisions together, and we eventually find common ground even if sometimes I don't entirely agree. We still have our separate departments or areas of responsibility based on our areas of expertise. The only time I exercise my veto right is when I absolutely know that my viewpoint is the correct way to go based on my many years in business.

I no longer need to be right every time. In fact, I know I'm not right every time, and I'm okay with that. I guess that's the difference between a strong and a fragile ego. Over the years my ego has evolved and become substantially stronger than it used to be. Remember, the fragile ego is at the root of partnership problems. A strong ego is the cement that can make a partnership thrive for many, many years.

You may ask yourself whether it's wise to go into a partnership in the first place, even if it's structured properly. Quite simply, the disadvantage of a partnership is that you'll share everything, including profits. The advantage of a partnership is the same: you'll share everything, good and bad. In the end I would advise you to consider this. A partnership provides leverage to go places that are often out of reach when you are running the show alone, and I'm referring mostly to the size of your company. You can build quicker with partners for several reasons. My last business was a gold-buying business, and at its peak we had 50 locations, something I would probably not have strived for had I been without partners.

Here is another vital partnership lesson: Aside from having additional hands in the fire to do the work, I think there's a more compelling reason to have one or more partners. It's not just that we all have different areas of expertise; more importantly, we all have different likes and dislikes. There's always some area within your business where you may not like to work. For some people it may be finances and accounting; for others it may be whatever manual labor is involved. It may also be something like sitting in government offices for hours every time you need a new license.

In my last business the division of labor went along the lines of expertise and likes. The issue of expertise is obvious, but the issue of likes may not be. The point is this: If there's something you don't like doing, then that area will almost certainly hold back your growth potential because you'll avoid it at all cost. But for your partner it may be the opposite. It may be the exact area where they like working, and they'll never procrastinate doing what's needed in that area. This is very important to take into consideration. You can often go much farther with partners than without them. But you have to do it right. Make sure every department has someone leading it with final authority in case of disagreement, and make sure that every partner's area of expertise and the activities that they enjoy doing correspond with the departments they are in charge of. Follow these simple ingredients to give your partnership a genuine chance to thrive.

Lesson #2

Dead on arrival business planning mistakes

Dead on arrival business planning mistakes

I've written dozens of business plans for individuals and groups seeking to start a business and/or raise money. A business plan is a vital ingredient for success and indispensable when it comes to raising capital. There are two reasons for this. For the investor, it shows a vision and a concept, a road map to profitability, viability of concept, financial projections, and more. It also shows that the concept and plan have been carefully thought through, enabling the plan to demonstrate how and when the requested investment will generate an acceptable return.

For company owners, the business planning process is an outstanding tool for engineering and analyzing their concept and turning it into a viable plan. An idea is simply not enough. There has to be a plan to take you from concept to fruition. The plan is your treasure map; creating your business plan is the same as finding the map to your treasure.

Most business plan writers give the business owner a questionnaire to fill out. I always did this so that I could accurately reflect the owner's idea and plan. But more importantly, I also did this because the questionnaire forces the business owners to think through their idea in detail. If the idea has not been adequately engineered into a workable plan, then the process of business planning can turn a good idea into a realistic and workable plan for success *where previously there was nothing more than an idea.*

During several years of writing business plans and assisting my clients in raising many millions of dollars in private start-up capital, I noticed that there were two types of clients who were destined to fail from the very beginning. Their business was dead on arrival, not because the central idea wasn't viable, but because the owners made two very common mistakes. I explain these here so that you can avoid them.

The first was that some of my clients planned themselves right out of existence. In essence they never put their plan into motion. They spent their entire time, sometimes many months or even years, going to seminars, attending meetings, planning this or planning that, and generally being professional busybodies. There was endless market research, focus group studies, meetings with vendors, and anything else they could think of. There was always one more thing to do before they were ready to take real action. When that was done, something else would crop up. It never ended, and their businesses never got off the ground. These people should learn to live by a sign I once saw on a sales manager's desk: "Do not confuse effort with results."

In essence the individuals I describe tried to create the perfect plan ahead of time. But there's no such thing. Things change. Unforeseeable events come up. Markets change. Customer needs change. Competition changes. Everything changes. The only permanent thing we have is change. All you need is a good plan and the ability to adapt and be flexible. You don't need a perfect plan. It doesn't exist anyway. Your plan will change as you move ahead with your project. That's an absolute guarantee.

I'm the exact opposite of what I just described. In each of my ventures, I leapt into action long before my plan was done. In fact, I jumped in before I even knew much about the business I was going into. I learned and developed a plan along the way. That's definitely not a viable strategy for everyone, but for me it became a unique formula that has worked repeatedly. However, the opposite never works because if you don't take that first concrete step, then nothing follows.

So what's the root of the problem when someone never stops planning and never takes real action to get moving? My guess is that it's fear, probably fear of failure. It would seem that these individuals are trying to be perfectionists, but businesses never get built on a perfect foundation. I don't believe that there's any such thing as planning for every single eventuality and having complete and perfect knowledge of everything to do with your project. It's also not necessary. Action is what is necessary.

Look at it this way: A trip to the moon or interplanetary travel, manned or unmanned, is an example of mankind's most complex endeavor. Most people believe that sending a rocket to the moon or to Mars involves a pre-calculated trajectory that has to be accurate to an incredible degree to succeed. But that's not how it works. The journey of a spaceship involves endless course corrections. If we're headed to the moon, then we continually adjust our course back and forth. Getting it approximately right along the way is good enough.

Once we have the moon in front of us, it's kind of hard to miss because of its size, although landing in the right spot does require a high degree of accuracy. But getting to the moon does not require perfect accuracy. You launch and point your spaceship in the general direction of the moon. Once you veer too far to the left, you course correct to the right. Fly too far to the right and you course correct to the left. This happens hundreds or thousands of times along the way.

Airplanes fly on the same principle. It's an endless process of course correction. A business is no different. You learn and adjust along the way. New information may come up. Assumptions may have to change. New ideas may improve on your previous plan. Any number of things can cause you to make changes. This is normal and should be welcomed. Adapt, adjust, and welcome change. It's inevitable anyway.

If you're looking to create the perfect plan that will be executed in every detail just like you anticipate, you're in for a surprise. That's never going to happen. Likewise, the concept of planning for every eventuality ahead of time will mean that you'll never be ready. There's always another eventuality to take into consideration, another seminar to attend, or another vendor to interview. You need to take action now. Don't spin your wheels until you literally run out of energy and enthusiasm. Start now. You're ready today. This does not mean that planning and preparation should stop. It never does. But using planning and preparation as a permanent substitute for action will not get you anywhere. You're just letting your fears push you into a false sense of security by making you feel productive when in fact you're just the opposite. You're procrastinating what really counts and substituting it with endless training.

Consider a race car driver who plays video games until he hits the perfect score, which no one ever does, rather than getting onto the track in a real race car and pushing the pedal to the metal. A credo I've always lived by is that there's only one way to get something done and that is to do it.

The second dead-on-arrival mistake people make is also something I witnessed repeatedly while writing business plans for a living. It's a scenario I encountered endless times while interviewing or being interviewed by prospective clients for business planning. We would sit down and I'd ask to hear their idea.

The conversation was often the same. Their basic business idea was typically decent. Let's say it was an idea in the telecommunications arena that involves a unique twist on calling cards. What followed was almost the exact same thing every time. The first thing they told me was along the lines of, "The telecom industry is a $2.1 trillion industry. If we get just a quarter of one percent of that business, we'll have revenues of $50 billion!" Uh huh, right. Go on. This sounds very familiar. I already knew what they would tell me next. "And that's not all. We'll generate revenues from calling cards and cell phones and selling our mailing lists and advertising and toll-free services and this and that." By that time I wanted someone to hyperspace me out of the meeting because this group had no idea what they were doing. They would never generate a dime of revenue from anything. Let me explain.

Virtually every great business created in the history of the world has always had one thing in common: They learned to do one thing, either new or different, and they learned to do it really, really well, often better than anyone else. They concentrated on that one idea that would set them apart, and that single-minded focus is what gave them the maximum chance for success. The rule is to do only one thing, but do it better than anyone else.

Focus is what's required in business. You need to focus on the one thing you're passionate about and then do it without distraction.

Whenever someone shows up with thirty-two different revenue sources and they want you to invest in their plan, run, run fast, and run far. They'll never succeed. They're inexperienced dreamers, and they have no idea what makes a business successful.

It should be noted that being a dreamer is not the same as being a visionary like Steve Jobs of Apple or Elon Musk of PayPal and Tesla Motors. Real visionaries are there to revolutionize an industry with single-minded focus on a single product, service, or better way of doing something. Their goal is not to make billions from a combination of multiple businesses thrown into one. Steve Jobs' vision was to create the most user-friendly and best-designed consumer electronics ever. He started with the Macintosh computer until that was perfected. Only then did he move on to Apple's next product. It was never about money. The money just naturally follows.

One could make a counterargument and say that Richard Branson of the Virgin group of companies was not focused on one thing, yet he still became stunningly successful. He has an airline, a record label, and dozens of other companies in a variety of fields. But Richard Branson is really not different from what I'm describing. His vision was to find an industry that lacked customer service or did not provide a positive and memorable customer experience. He wanted to change that. And that's exactly what he did in one industry, with single-minded focus. When he succeeded, he found another and did the same thing. This is how companies can develop multiple sources of income. You become the best at one thing, and once you've succeeded, you can expand or diversify. This is not the same as going into it with a shotgun approach by attempting to collect from everything at once. Once Steve Jobs succeeded in the computer business, he moved on to other consumer electronics and applied the same formula, from the iPod and iPhone to Apple TV and more. They are all beautifully designed inside and out, and simpler to use than any other group of consumer electronics have ever been. But each was introduced individually, and none followed until the last introduction became successful.

The key is to find your niche and stick with it without distraction. Don't try to be everything to everyone and thereby lose focus. Do one thing and do it really, really well. Once you succeed, you can add on a new product or service. Once that is successful, you can repeat the process. Then, once you've decided how you're going to make your mark, get moving. Don't plan yourself out of existence. Every journey starts with a single step. If you don't take that first step, you'll never get to the next steps. Just do it.

Lesson #3

Loose lips sink ships!

Loose lips sink ships!

Years ago I lived in Boca Raton, Florida, for just under one year. I was hired by a group of investors there to run a direct-mail sweepstakes promotional company. Sweepstakes was my expertise at the time, and I was one of the best creative minds in the business. Our industry consisted of a tight-knit group of only about ten companies, yet collectively we mailed in excess of 20 to 30 million pieces of mail per month. After about ten months I decided to leave Florida because I didn't particularly care for the ethics, or lack thereof, of this group so I made plans to return to California.

When our competition heard of my plans to leave, I was made several job offers immediately. The largest company by far in our business was located in Orange County, California. They made me an offer that was to be my crowning achievement in this particular industry. I was offered a vice-presidential position with a salary of $250,000 plus bonuses. This was during the late '80s when the value of such an offer was enormous.

As I packed and prepared to move, I told one of my closest acquaintances in our industry about where I was going. He was a competitor but also a friend. I was elated and wanted to share my good fortune with someone. When I got to Orange

County, I called my new employer only to be told that they could no longer consider hiring me. Imagine moving across the country to find out the job offer you were moving for was suddenly retracted.

What happened turned out to be my own fault. The acquaintance with whom I shared my good fortune told someone else, and soon the whole industry knew. This happened in a matter of days. I didn't find out about this until I had already arrived in Orange County.

Here's what happened: When several of my new employer's largest competitors found out about my planned move to join the industry leader, they felt so threatened by this merger that they in turn threatened to cut them off from exchanging mailing lists. This was considered death in our industry because the livelihood of any direct-mail company is tied to the quality of the mailing lists it has access to. In our close-knit group of semi-friendly competition, we exchanged lists with each other and negotiated priority positioning on these lists. Without these lists and prime positioning, millions in revenues would vanish. My employer had no choice but to retract the offer it made me, and I moved to Orange County to no job.

The lesson I learned was simple: loose lips sink ships. I indirectly let my competition know about my plans, and they maneuvered to counteract the perceived competitive threat. I had no one to blame but myself for revealing my new job opportunity to my friend.

Information may be power, but withholding information can be even more powerful. Keep your information to yourself so that people don't know your secrets. Everything you say and reveal will be used against you. The less your competition, vendors, or employees know about your plans and activities, the better it is for you. Keep them guessing as to what you're up to. It keeps them from outmaneuvering you, and it keeps them from copying what you are doing.

The more secrets your adversaries think you have, the better positioned you are to gain their respect and admiration. Even if you have no secrets and even if what you do is simple and easily duplicated, don't let anyone know this. It's only easy once you know how something is done, so don't let anyone know how you do it. Let them think you have special skills and an unknown perceived advantage.

If you give away your information, you give away your advantage. Sometimes that advantage is merely perceived, but perception is reality. A perceived advantage is no less important than an actual strategic advantage. Opening your mouth at the wrong time can cost you dearly — as I learned.

It's tempting to talk about our good fortune. It's human to want to share your good fortune with others. But others aren't always happy about our successes, especially when our success makes them appear less successful in comparison. Therefore be humble about your achievements, and don't talk about them until they're completed.

As Bono from U2 tells us in one of his songs, "If you want to kiss the sky, you'd better learn how to kneel." Some interpret this as getting down on your knees to pray in order to reach heaven, but I believe it also means that if you want to achieve greatness, you need to learn humility. This is a profound lesson.

Humility is golden for several reasons. First, you don't want to reveal your secrets, your moves, your information, or your progress because it can and will be used against you. Reveal your plans, and you'll give away your strategic advantage.

The second reason is that if you gloat, you'll create resentment. This makes the temptation for an adversary to harm you that much more satisfying. Nobody likes a braggart or a show-off. I know I don't, and I quickly shut them out when I'm faced by one. As a business owner and employer, a vendor who tells me over and over again how great they are won't get my business. Likewise, an employee who tells me repeatedly how awesome they are and all the great things they have done for my company gets shut out from future opportunity. I know when an employee is great. It's my job to know. I don't need to be told.

It's uncomfortable to have to listen to someone who shows off or brags. If the braggart has no relevance to my life or business, then I make sure they disappear from my life altogether. But there is a way you can impress me if that's really your purpose. You can impress me by trying really hard not to impress me. Be humble. As an accomplished businessman I know my employees' and vendors' achievements without having to be told. Like I said, it's my job to know. When someone insists on telling me, it cancels their achievement in my mind. It also causes me to doubt whether they actually achieved what they claim.

We can never earn respect and recognition by requesting it or demanding it. Respect and recognition for our achievements are earned by doing and by setting an example for others to follow. People automatically know and respond accordingly. If a humble person achieves success, everyone loves to reward them. If a braggart succeeds and proceeds to throw it in our face, we end up punishing them despite their achievement.

We react in a similarly harsh manner when recognition and respect for achievement is demanded from us, which is all linked to integrity. Integrity isn't something you talk about. It's something you do. In fact, true integrity is found in what you do that's good when no one's watching. As a side note, I've also learned to avoid any company with the word "Integrity" in it. Never has a single one of them lived up to their name.

Loose lips sink ships. It's a fact of life. Silence is often your best strategy as it denies your competition the ammunition they seek to harm you.

Lesson #4

The only way to predict the future is to create it

The only way to predict the future is to create it

This chapter could be considered the most important chapter in this book as it gives you the tools to achieve virtually anything you desire — and this includes all those dreams you have that may seem impossible to you now.

This chapter is on goal setting. Admittedly much of the information in this chapter can be found elsewhere. There are books on how to set goals available in any bookstore. The reasons I'm including it here is that it's vitally important information and my life has been a product of goal setting and knowing how to realize them.

I've learned several invaluable methods for making my goals come true and have proven the effectiveness of my techniques over and over again. This is the best of the best on goal setting. So what I'm going to share with you is not goal-setting theory. It's a summation of those methods that I've tried, tested, and distilled down into techniques that work beyond your wildest imagination.

It helps to know that in every study ever done on what habits set successful people apart from poor people, the top two are virtually *always* setting goals and using "To Do" lists. How many poor people do you know who set goals or make "To Do" lists other than grocery lists? Probably not a single one. That's because if they did, they wouldn't be poor.

"To Do" lists are an integral part of being productive and can also be incorporated into the fulfillment of your goals. I always have several "To Do" lists I work on at any one time. I've done this my whole life and can't even fathom functioning productively without them. I have them on paper, in Outlook, on my iPhone, and on my iPad. They can be daily tasks or specific to a project, such as a new business venture. Either way, if it's something that needs to be done, then it needs to be written down on a list. As I complete tasks, I check them off my list. New tasks get added to my lists almost daily.

Before we delve into the art of goal setting, I'll share a little trick with you in regards to "To Do" lists. I'm doing this because I wholeheartedly believe in the importance of using "To Do" lists, and they're an integral part of achieving your goals. Here it is: *Do what you like least, first.* Think about it. Whether we're active in using written "To Do" lists, or we just have a list of daily tasks in our mind, everyone always pushes out what they don't like doing for as long as possible. The problem with this is that you're going through your entire day knowing in the back of your mind that you still have to do something you don't like doing. What does this do to your mood during the day?

Now imagine if you completed that same unpleasant task first thing in the morning. The rest of your day would be much brighter knowing you have only pleasant tasks ahead.

It makes you happier and more productive. Furthermore, if something has to be done, pleasant or unpleasant, then you might as well do it right away; otherwise, you're wasting time. It has to be done anyway. Every time you push something around on your desk to be completed later, you're wasting time during the act of moving it aside or thinking about doing it later. You lose time and productivity.

In the big picture, if you don't master the art of goal setting, including using "To Do" lists, the other lessons are a waste of time. Goal setting and knowing how to realize your goals are the foundation for everything else. If you master the goal-setting techniques I'm about to share with you, you can achieve virtually anything.

There's only one way to predict the future, and that's to create it. It's true; the best way to predict the future is to create it. This is done through the awesome power of knowing how to properly set goals and knowing how to apply certain techniques for making them come true. We don't have to live according to the circumstances in our lives. We can create our own circumstances, ones that we choose.

Nothing compares to the power of goal setting when it comes to achieving the future that you want for yourself and your family. But you have to know how to do it properly. I promise you that this chapter on goal setting is unlike any you may have ever read before because it's entirely the result of techniques that are tried and proven to work. I don't claim originality for these techniques, only for choosing the best of what's out there and consequently what has worked for me.

Let's start with the obvious. You have to set goals and create a plan if you want to succeed. Goal setting isn't one of those things you hear about but never do although you intuitively know you should. You *really* need to do it. That's lesson one. You need to set goals, period. Why? Because goal setting works.

Some people confuse goals with dreams. A goal and a dream are not the same thing. It's okay to dream, for if you don't have any dreams, how are you going to make your dreams come true? But you have to convert your dreams into goals if you want to achieve them. *A goal is a dream with a deadline.* To reach your goal by your deadline, you need to have a plan. You need to plan your work, and then you need to work your plan. Now reread this paragraph. There's a lot of important information in these few lines.

How you arrive at your plan is what this chapter is all about.

I use two methods of goal setting depending on the type of goal I'm pursuing, the baby-step method and the best-path method. I also call them the conscious and subconscious methods. Both of them work so incredibly well that they have the power to change your life virtually overnight. Learn to use them both and you become unstoppable.

The baby-step method or conscious method involves creating a detailed plan that can be easily followed step-by-step regardless of how big your goal is. The theory is this: Imagine I asked you to build a pyramid the size of a small Egyptian pyramid. Needless to say, that would sound like a daunting task. But consider this: What if you broke the task down into small achievable steps, such as placing one brick on the ground at a time, even just a few bricks a day, every day, until completion? What would happen? What first appeared to be a pipe dream has now turned into an achievable goal. You've broken a large goal into lots of manageable little tasks. I call them baby steps to illustrate they're small enough that anyone can do them.

You can do this with almost any goal. The key is to break down big steps into smaller steps. Then break those smaller steps into even smaller steps, or baby steps. When the steps are so small that each one of them is ridiculously easy to achieve and you don't deviate from the path, then your goal comes within reach. It's only a matter of taking one baby step after another until you're done. It's that simple, and all those dozens or hundreds of baby steps will add up to your goal. If you lay down one brick at a time, even just a few bricks each day, sooner or later you'll have an impressive pyramid in your backyard.

Here's how it works in practice: Take your major goal and break it down into smaller manageable steps, then break each one of those into even smaller steps, or baby steps. You need to do this in writing and add a deadline to each of the larger steps. First, write down your goal and when you want to have it completed. That is, add your deadline. Be specific with what you want to achieve. Describe it in every detail. Then break it down into multiple steps. Take each of those steps and break them down into as many smaller steps as needed until it's obvious that each individual step is easily fulfilled. Once completed, your list of baby steps will be very similar

Parviz Firouzgar

to a "To Do" list. It's only a matter of doing them and sticking to your schedule.

Each plan will be different, and, depending on your goal, you'll sense how many steps and how many tiers are needed. When all the smallest steps are ridiculously easy to achieve, you'll have created a plan you can follow. Altogether your steps will add up to your goal, and if you complete them one after another, they'll get you there.

You are creating a consciously predetermined path with many tiny achievable steps so that you know exactly where you're going and how you're going to get there. You'll simply put one foot in front of the other until you get from A to B along the path you've outlined for yourself.

Let's say your goal is to open a business of a certain type by a certain date. Let's also assume that one of the first larger steps in your plan is to create a business entity, such as a corporation or an LLC. You would then break down that step into smaller steps as outlined below:

Describe your goal and determine an exact deadline for completion – define your goal in detail. In this case it might be opening a new business and being operational in six months.

Major step (create business entity)   Deadline
- Smaller step (decide on type of entity)
     1. Baby step (discuss with attorney)
     2. Baby step (get recommendations from other business owners)
     3. Baby step (research types of entities on Internet)

-54-

- Smaller step (determine in what state to create entity)
    1. Baby step (research prices)
    2. Baby step (get advice from other business owners)
    3. Baby step (discuss with attorney)

<u>Major step</u> (develop marketing plan)   Deadline
- Smaller step (prepare budget)
    1. Baby step (research what competitors are doing)
    2. Baby step (get marketing proposals from vendors)
    3. Etc., etc.

You then do the same for every other major step in your plan. This may include sales strategies, product development, business planning, etc. You break each major step down into smaller steps, and if necessary, break those down again into baby steps. Every major step should have a completion date so that you create a true step-by-step road map that will take you to your goal.

Baby steps are completed first and eventually lead to the completion of more significant steps. In deciding the type of entity to create, after talking to your attorney, other successful business owners, and doing some of your own research online, you can then make an informed decision thereby completing your first significant step. Your next step is to decide what state to create the entity in by using the same process.

Completed baby steps will add up to the completion of major steps, and the completion of all major steps will add up to accomplishing your goal. This method is very simple in design and execution, but as you'll see later, it's not suitable for all types of goals, only those where you can create a clearly defined *predetermined* path.

The more structure you put into your plan, the more predictable the outcome will be. However, flexibility with deadlines, changing items to be completed, and additions and deletions should be expected, as long as there's a valid reason for making those changes. As your knowledge of business conditions evolves, so should the steps in your plan. Procrastination is not a valid reason for altering your plan or deadlines.

Never abandon your list. It's like a treasure map. If you follow it faithfully, you'll eventually get to your treasure. An important component of what you'll be doing is to look at your list several times per day to remind yourself of what you want to achieve and what still needs to be done. Your goal needs to have a permanent presence in your mind. To achieve this, simply reviewing your list morning, day, and night will enhance your success curve for reasons you'll understand in more detail as you continue reading. You'll be implanting your goal firmly into your mind until it becomes a part of you.

The baby-step system is about creating a predetermined path to get from A to B with some flexibility if changes need to be made along the way. That's why I also call it the conscious method. You are consciously deciding what path to take. But what happens when your goal doesn't lend itself easily to creating a path, or what if there are multiple paths and you don't know which one's best? Or what if you have no idea at all what your path should be, even when there doesn't seem to be a path to choose from? This is where an even more powerful technique enters the picture, the best-path method.

The best-path or subconscious method is dramatically different from the baby-step method, and the foundation for this method is the most awesome technique for achieving success ever discovered. If you learn only one thing in your life, this should be it. You can create anything by applying this stunningly effective means for achieving real results. Failure will cease to be an option in your life.

Ninety percent of our mind's activity operates on the subconscious level. Only 10 percent is in the conscious realm. If the baby-step or conscious method uses the conscious 10 percent of our mind to achieve powerful and predictable results, just imagine what the subconscious method can achieve if it uses the other 90 percent of our mind.

Your mind is like an iceberg where only one-tenth is visible above water and nine-tenths is submerged. The visible portion of the mind is the conscious portion. The invisible portion is the subconscious, which, like an iceberg, is vastly larger and more powerful than the visible portion. Imagine the untapped potential of your subconscious mind. I'll teach you next how to utilize your unlimited subconscious potential.

To illustrate the results that are attainable with this method, I'm going to offer a real example from my life. This will show you only the goal and the results, not the actual method or the steps you need to take to make the system work. We'll get to that soon enough.

One of my passions in life has always been cars. I love to drive, and if I'm driving a car that I love, I'm a happy camper. When I first discovered the best-path method, I immediately began using it to get the cars that I wanted. At the beginning I had no idea how incredibly effective this technique was. The results amazed me repeatedly. Over the years I owned every single car I ever imagined having, all the way up to a Lamborghini and a Bentley. In fact, if my next dream car was beyond my financial means, then my means would quickly rise up to meet the purchasing power I needed to buy the car that I desired.

Here's what I did many years ago: It started when I wanted a white 1990 convertible Corvette. I put a picture of one on the wall above my desk in the exact color and style I desired. I then applied the best-path method of goal setting. Less than one year later I found myself driving a 1990 convertible Corvette, essentially identical to the one in the picture above my desk at work. One year or so later I wanted a Lexus LS400 sedan, so I repeated the same procedure. I hung a picture in a place where I would see it every day. At that time I was building a mail-order company. I had an investor who was also the majority owner of the company. After just one year he was well on target for making a profit of over a million dollars from my company, so he surprised me with a brand-new $54,000 Lexus LS400 for my birthday. Amazingly it was the exact color I wanted, pearl white. I'll never forget that surprise.

Another year later I noticed a blank spot on the wall above my desk, so I decided to fill it with a picture of the new S-Class Mercedes that had just been released. It didn't take long before I was able to write a check for $94,000 to buy a Mercedes 500 SEL. After I was happily driving around in this dreamboat of a car, a landmark event occurred that became one of those learning experiences that led to this book. I was doing exceedingly well in my first really successful company, and I thought I could do no wrong. That's when I started making a few mistakes.

Primarily, I started to identify with material objects. My cars became the measure for my success and an integral part of my image. If you looked at the space above my desk at that time, you would have seen the picture of the 500 SEL replaced by a 600 SEL, an unnecessary distraction from my business activities. It took only one year before I upgraded to this twelve-cylinder monster, and I was still only around thirty years old.

Today, many years and many lessons later, I still have expensive toys, but I enjoy them for what they are, not for the perceived image they provide. I don't identify with them, nor do I fear losing them. I'm a different person.

So what's the best-path or subconscious method of goal setting and how does it work? The basic premise is that where the baby-step method assumes that we know the path from A to B and can therefore plan it out with numerous small sequential steps, the path we may choose toward some goals may not be the most efficient, fastest, or most cost-effective path. In fact, even if we have several paths to choose from, there may be others out there we don't know about. We may also be faced with a situation where we see no path at all. Many goals are abandoned because of this precise reason.

This is where we let our subconscious do the work for us. It's not only capable of finding a path all on its own; it's capable of finding the most efficient path and getting us there. It can even find a path when our conscious mind doesn't see one at all.

Your mind has untapped powers beyond your wildest imagination. Unleashing those powers does take some effort and self-discipline, but the effort is well worth it. All forms of riches, from health to wealth, begin from a single source, and from only this source — your mind. Unleashing this transformative power happens singularly via disciplining yourself to control what goes through your mind — by training yourself to think the right kind of thoughts.

When one is capable of training one's mind to think the right thoughts in the correct manner, those thoughts will inevitably transform into their material counterpart, creating whatever one has mentally conceived. It's an absolute law of the universe. Whatever you think so shall you become. Numerous books have been written on this topic, including the most famous self-improvement book of all, *Think and Grow Rich* by Napoleon Hill.

In the same way that positive thoughts can transform into their material counterparts, negative thoughts will also transform into reality, and that's why most people live miserable lives. Their lives are literally the result of their thoughts and the individual's complete lack of any ability to discipline their mind. This also tells us that we already have everything we need to become healthy, wealthy, and wise. Many of us just don't know that we possess such power, nor do most of us know how to use and unleash this limitless power within. Realistically, even if we all did know about this power, most people are just unwilling to make the necessary effort to learn how to use it.

Men spend their entire lives seeking fame and fortune without ever attaining either, never realizing that the source is within. The formula is so simple, yet its implementation requires some effort. In the best-path method, the conscious mind determines what it wants to create; the subconscious then goes to work creating it once it's set in motion using the right technique.

Implementing this goal-setting technique requires a clear definition of your goal, a burning desire to achieve it, clear intent that you'll achieve it, concentration, belief, tension, letting go, and regular repetition. We'll go through each of these steps as you'll need to implement them in the order described. Initially, this technique will require some effort and self-discipline as you'll be retraining your mind. However, once you master the sequence, it will become second nature, and achieving all your goals will become an integral part of your being.

The secret to the best-path method is using a universal law called entropy. In simple terms it means that everything in the universe seeks to move toward a state of equilibrium.

Maximum entropy is akin to a state of equilibrium. In the second law of thermodynamics, for example, heated matter will dissipate heat until it reaches a state of balance with its surroundings where it will neither cool down further nor seek an increase in its heat or energy. When a body is in a high state of energy (hot), surrounded by air in a lower state of energy (cool), then a form of tension is in place that seeks to move both toward a state of equilibrium. It's a move from disorder to order.

Everything in nature moves toward equilibrium. When there's tension, that tension cannot last. It has to move to a state of resolution or equilibrium. Knowing this, we can use it to our advantage. *If we strategically set up tension in a way where its resolution equals the fulfillment of our goals, then we have discovered and used a law of the universe to our advantage.*

One of the pioneers in discovering and defining this method is Robert Fritz in his landmark best-selling book *The Path of Least Resistance*. In it he refers to the tension I describe as structural tension. I cannot give enough praise and credit to this outstanding achievement. For me, his method was life changing.

In the same way that a question seeks an answer, a goal seeks fulfillment. The goal only needs to be at the receiving end of a system of tension that you'll set up in your mind. As hot becomes cool, where you are will become where you want to be. In fact, that's the secret. If you can separately define where you are and where you want to be, that very act of articulating those two states of being will begin to create the tension we seek. It only needs to be done according to some specific guidelines I'll share with you here.

Allow me to repeat a phrase from earlier in this chapter. *Implement this goal-setting technique requires a clear definition of your goal, a burning desire to achieve it, clear intent that you'll achieve it, concentration, belief, tension, letting go, and regular repetition.* The only thing missing from this list is a clear definition of where you are now. You need this to create the tension that makes this system work.

Your first step is to define your goal. Be clear about what you want. Be specific and describe your desired outcome in its entirety. Do it in writing. Conclude your description with a deadline for the achievement of your goal. For this method to work, your goal has to be something you really want, and whatever effort is required to achieve it or gain it becomes irrelevant. You'll do whatever it takes.

Consider that if you asked almost anyone if they'd like to be a black belt in karate, virtually everyone would say yes. Then why aren't they black belts? Why haven't they made the effort to take lessons to fulfill their desire? The truth is they don't want to be a black belt badly enough; otherwise, they would be one. That's not true desire; that's wishful thinking. Your goal has to be a burning desire, something you get emotional over, because the subconscious mind gives preference to those conscious thoughts that are accompanied by emotion and those that dominate as a result of repetition. Emotion will enhance the tension that seeks resolution. We'll discuss repetition shortly.

After defining a goal that you really, really want, next you'll define where you are now, your current reality. Again, do it in writing. This isn't as easy as it sounds because we don't always see our current reality objectively. You need to describe your current state as close to the way things actually are, good or bad, without letting skewed perceptions influence your description. If you're sick and your goal is to get healthy, don't make your illness sound less serious or worse than it is. Describe it exactly as it is, whatever state that may be.

You've now defined where you are and where you want to be. If you have a burning desire to get from one to the other, you've already set up the required tension.

You'll now tell yourself to get from one to the other. "I hereby intend to get from here (describe current reality) to there (goal) by this date (your deadline)." Concentrate as you do this and show resolve. Tell your subconscious to solve the problem and get you from A to B, but don't try to influence your mind to follow a certain path. Let your subconscious decide the path for you.

Most importantly, you have to believe that it will work. Believe it and it will work.

Maybe you've heard the famous phrase, *"Whatever the mind can conceive and believe, the mind can achieve."* Notice that it doesn't say only what the mind can conceive it can achieve. It clearly says conceive AND believe. You have to have faith in your mind's ability. You have to see it already happening in your mind. Visualize the outcome and know that your mind has powers beyond our comprehension.

The power of belief can also be found in scripture. Mark 11:24 states, "Therefore I tell you, whatever you ask for in prayer, believe that you have received it, and it will be yours." This is powerful information. The Bible is telling you that you have to believe that what you pray for has already been granted to you, and then you'll receive it.

You've now set up the tension that seeks resolution. That resolution, toward a state of equilibrium (or maximum entropy), is the fulfillment of your goal.

It's vital that you refrain from telling your mind how to get from A to B. Let your subconscious decide. Let it find the best path for you as it inevitably will, every time. It will probably be a path you never dreamed of, one that's filled with unexpected events and welcome coincidences. Let the universe conspire to make your dream come true. Believe it and it will happen. I've used this method countless times and have yet to see it fail. If it does fail, then the ingredients of burning desire and belief were probably missing. It doesn't work for wishful thinking. It works for everything that you truly want.

Now let go. Stop thinking about your goal for the remainder of the day and night. Let your subconscious mind do the work it knows how to do so well. Let the tension resolve by allowing your subconscious to create a path toward your goal — that is, toward equilibrium.

There's only one other step, repetition. After a period of letting go, repeat the above exercise to reinforce your desire. Then let go again. Repeat every day or every few days. Then let your subconscious go to work uninterrupted once again. Watch miracles happen.

Here is a great day-to-day application of a simplified version of the best-path method that we've all seen happen in our lives. We've all used it when we forget a name or when we need to find a solution to a problem. All the conscious effort we put into remembering the forgotten name or finding a problem's solution rarely offers immediate results. But what invariably happens hours later, oftentimes waking us up in the middle of the night? The answer suddenly appears out of the blue! We've all experienced this. It appears that while our conscious mind couldn't remember or solve the problem, all the mental effort engaged our subconscious to start working on the issue at hand. It continues to work on the problem in the background until it's solved.

Over time, I've turned this method of remembering or problem solving into a very reliable skill. The results make me smile every time. It seems that the more conscious effort we put into a problem or a lost memory, the more vigorously our subconscious takes over when we let go. And that's the key — make a concerted, conscious effort and then let go completely. Let your subconscious go to work without conscious interference. Your effort serves to engage the other 90 percent of your brain.

By applying the conscious (baby-step) and subconscious (best-path) methods of goal setting, you can achieve anything you desire, even those goals that seem completely out of reach. Learn these two methods and watch your life transform into a powerhouse of achievement.

Live a life of setting and achieving goals. Make your dreams come true by setting deadlines and thereby turning dreams into goals. Know where you are, where you want to go, and what you want to achieve. As Basil S. Walsh said, *"If you don't know where you are going, how can you expect to get there?"*

Lesson #5

You're not ready to be the boss ... until you understand this lesson!

You're not ready to be the boss ... until you understand this lesson!

"If you want to kiss the sky, you'd better learn how to kneel."
As I previously mentioned, I believe Bono and U2's
prophetic lyrics can be interpreted two ways. The first has
religious overtones: if you want to go to heaven, you'd better
first learn to kneel — that is, obey and submit to your God
and master. The second is more earthly and relevant to this
text: if you want to achieve greatness, you need to learn
humility first.

Have you ever had a nine-to-five job where you were
convinced that your boss was inept, egotistical, and utterly
unqualified for his position of authority? Moreover, weren't
you convinced that you could do a better job ... if only
they'd give you the opportunity? You knew you'd make a
great boss, at least better than him.

This is the plight of countless people across the world.
Salespeople are a perfect example. You're doing an
exemplary job from morning till night, and you know your
contribution to the company is significant. Your superiors
recognize you although they don't acknowledge your
contribution nearly enough. As you toil away, day to day,
you watch your boss benefit from the fruits of your labor. If

he's a sales manager, then he derives his income directly from the sales that YOU make. Moreover, your boss spends the majority of his time running from one meeting to another and walking around acting important. The rest of his time is spent telling people what to do, complaining there isn't enough production, and politicking within the company so that he can advance to an even less stressful position. You and the rest of the troops keep this schmuck in a $100,000 Mercedes while you drive a Honda. His problem: Getting a bigger budget so that he can hire more salespeople so that he can make more money so that he can buy another toy he doesn't need. Your problem: Making enough sales to support your family and keep your job.

You can do better than your boss. You know it. In your bones you can feel it. In fact, you should be the boss. After all, you know what it takes to ride people to work hard and produce more. You should be the one telling everyone what to do. At least you care about the customers, and more importantly, you know where the company's money comes from. It comes from its salespeople. And that's what this company could really use, someone who cares about the company's customers and sales force, not someone who cares only about his own job security and advancement.

You wait and you wait, wondering if any of these managers are ever going to leave. You would actually support one of them getting promoted so that their space in the corporate ladder would become available. You're dying to show them what a great job you can do. And then you wait some more.

Months, even years pass by, and then destiny finally reveals itself. One of the managers decides to move to Montana with his spouse to live the simpler life. The job opening is posted immediately in the lunch room. Lucky for you, your production has been great, and you get along well with the branch manager, your boss's boss, who's going to do the hiring. Fortunately he doesn't know that you think he's a spineless do-nothing who just sits around sipping coffee in his office all day.

The next step is for you to go to your manager to ask him what he thinks of you applying for the position. You're amped and ready to shine, itching to become the next manager-of-the-month wunderkind. He professes his enthusiastic support, failing to mention that only over his dead body would he ever contribute to losing your sales numbers on his team.

You walk into the branch manager's office to announce that you're ready to escape the sea of mediocrity surrounding you. You let him know to expect your resume. And then you hear those magic words, "I look forward to it." You may even succumb to temptation and ask whether anyone else is already being considered for the position. "No one." Yesss.

It's time to prepare. You're going to do what all managers who are one level above you should be doing and obviously never did. You're going to read a book on management.

The day of the interview arrives, and you walk out feeling pretty darn good about your chances. You call your family and tell them that you're going to make them very proud.

You tell them how the branch manager asked a few questions about your resume and then a few more "what would you do if" questions. You answered every one of his situational queries intelligently and creatively. You were even able to incorporate some of the management strategies you just read about in your answers.

There was only one instance where you felt you did not impress him, and that was when he hinted that usually they hire individuals for this position who have a college degree one level higher than you have. But you feel that you totally overcame that objection by explaining how hard you'll work and what a quick learner you are. The interview ends with an explanation that you'll be *seriously* considered. Did you remember telling him that you read *The One Minute Manager*? Oh yes, of course you did.

A few days pass and nothing happens. No one calls on you for another interview, and the wait is killing you. Soon you ask your manger if he's heard anything. All he knows is that you did well in the interview. And then a meeting is called the next day at noon. Everyone gathers, and you can barely contain yourself. Are they going to announce you at the meeting and ask you to come to the front of the room? You strategically place yourself in the aisle. Actually, this isn't feeling like such a sure thing after all, and who's the new suit in the room? He looks like he came straight out of IBM from twenty years ago.

In your entire life it has never been so hard for you to keep smiling as when the new manager is introduced. Where the hell did he come from? He looks like a male version of a

Stepford wife. What happened to the policy of promoting from within? This cannot be happening!

Does any of this feel familiar? Your circumstances probably aren't so different; only the details will vary from person to person. This is typically how it goes. You know you're ready. In fact, you know you can do better than your current boss. You just need a chance to prove it. Then why won't they give you the chance?

The truth is you're *not* ready. I know this because I found myself in the exact same position. I was a salesperson for six long years in a large corporation that loved my superstar sales performance but would promote me only to higher-ranking sales positions. Once they even made up a new title for me, and I've since forgotten how many times my title changed from this or that to "Senior" this or that, but never to manager.

Today, with 20/20 hindsight I know what I didn't know then. I wasn't ready. I wanted to be boss. I wanted the power. Now I know that this precise craving was proof that I wasn't ready. A good manager doesn't crave power. He knows that he works for his employees just as much as they work for him, and he acts accordingly, not by bossing people around but by leading by example.

You're not ready to be a good manager until you're able to be a good employee first and have no problem doing virtually any job, no matter how menial. A good manager will offer to make his secretary's coffee once in a while, or take the trash out. He never asks anyone to do something he's not willing to do himself.

You're also not ready to be boss until you realize that being boss doesn't mean you stop having to kiss up to someone. It's a tough concept for employees to grasp, but everyone reports to someone. It's not just your immediate superior but also the managers higher up; they answer to the executives. For the executives, it's the directors. For the directors, it's the company owners or shareholders. And for them, it's the customer. It's a circle.

Ultimately, the guy at the top reports to the guy at the bottom or, more accurately, to thousands of guys at the bottom. In simple terms, a manager or business owner reports directly to his or her employees and to the company's customers. He's not such a big boss after all. Seasoned managers know this, yet inexperienced employees will deny this. They'll say, "Sounds good, but I know better."

The worst mistake a company can make is to reward their star salesperson with a move into management. This often ends in disaster. The salesperson first has to know what it's like to be a manager, and he has to want the realities of such a position. Otherwise, his perceived image of management will simply not conform to reality. If he knew the truth, he may not want the position after all. There's wisdom in saying that we choose the kind of misery we enjoy the most. The problem is that you have to know what miseries lie ahead before you can actually know whether the move is right for you.

Many an excellent salesperson has been promoted to manager and is not only a failure at his new job, but feels miserable in his new position. It's simply not what he expected. In the end, this type of move often fails, and the salesperson ends up back in sales. All he got from the experience was a seriously bruised ego.

Managers and owners have just as many stresses, if not more, than their employees. They are just very different, and one of those differences is responsibilities. Employees often have no idea what it's like to walk around in their superior's shoes. Unbeknownst to the employee, their life is actually rather carefree compared to that of their superior. They may have never considered that the higher up you are, the more responsibility you have.

As a regular employee, your responsibility is ultimately only to your manager, yourself, and your family. The boss has responsibilities that include you and your family and dozens — or even hundreds — of other livelihoods. Believe it or not, they have a responsibility to you, just like you have to them. Then they have a responsibility toward their superiors and the company. If a company owner or manager fails in his duties, the ramifications can be disastrous to many lives. If you fail, you ultimately report only to yourself. This is why firing someone is so difficult. Any of us can mouth the words, but we know that when we have to do it, we actually do care for the person in front of us and we know the hardship we will put them through. Sometimes it's harder on the person doing the firing than the person being fired. Some people are just not cut out for such responsibilities as these.

Once management responsibilities are understood, then many would-be managers, owners, and entrepreneurs inevitably decline and stay where they are. Alternatively they'll enter into management or entrepreneurship much more prepared and therefore more effective.

So when are you ready to be boss, and if you're not ready yet, how can you make yourself ready? You're ready when you understand the following: You need to know the stresses that come with the territory, and you need to want those more than your current stresses. They'll be very different. You need to understand and want the responsibilities that will always be much greater than those you are dealing with now. You need to be willing to sacrifice relative carefree freedom for a series of rewards that may not be worth it to everyone. You definitely need to be humble in your new role, for it's humility that will allow you to become a more effective manager, a manager who leads by example rather than with the crack of a whip.

To be an effective manager you need know that you are still and always will be reporting to someone. You need to not feel superior over the people beneath you. Anyone who sees himself as "boss" is one who will have problems becoming as effective as he could be. A great boss is one who sees himself in a role of responsibility and service. In fact, this is true leadership — power with benevolence and without machismo or egotism.

Only experience will eventually tell you that you may not be ready right now to take the next step up, whether it's from employee to manager, or from manager to owner or entrepreneur. It gets harder as you move up the ladder, and the better you are at it, the easier you'll make it look. That's why so many people think they can fill their boss's shoes. The boss makes it look easy. What they don't realize is that a true master blends into the background so as to allow others to shine. He has attained so much personal power that he doesn't need to show it or even use it.

If you still think it gets easier as you move up, then you are simply not ready. If you think that a boss's primary function is to boss people around, then you are definitely not ready. If you can't wait to be the one calling the shots, you are probably a management disaster waiting to happen. And if you still don't believe me, please feel free to find out the hard way.

Another related move, equally fraught with pitfalls and analogous to one's first move into management, is moving from working within a company to starting your own company. No one explains this better than Michael Gerber in his groundbreaking book *The E-Myth* (i.e., The Entrepreneurial Myth). Among a long list of great business books, this one definitely ranks in the top ten.

In a nutshell, many people who do a fabulous job within a company soon come to the conclusion that if they've mastered the mechanics of the business — like the baker in a bakery shop — better than anyone, why shouldn't they just open a similar business for themselves and make substantially more money in the process?

Like a salesperson wanting to delve into the "easy life" of a manager, the employee-to-entrepreneur move can be equally paved with disappointment and disaster. The technical skills of an employee who handles the raw mechanics of a business are vastly different from the skill set required to run that same business.

As Michael Gerber accurately points out, most people who make this move never see an easier or more prosperous life. They end up working much longer hours for substantially less money than what they had before. The reason is that they lack the unique skills required to efficiently run a business, which are often invisible to the average employee and from which the misconception arises.

The skills required to run a business involve leadership, business and financial planning, accounting, strategizing, controlled risk taking, effectively managing people, and handling continuous pressures that no employee can even fathom.

How will an employee who has never been a senior manager or business owner react to a sudden downturn in his business, human resource problems, lawsuits, cash flow issues, or regulatory hurdles? That doesn't even include having to have adequate capital to fund the business and dedicating long hours every night to building the business until it's actually making a profit.

Entrepreneurs and business owners are a very unique breed of people. They frequently make this professional choice because they literally have no choice in the matter. It's in their blood to take risks, create something out of nothing, and build something to be proud of. The sacrifices they have to make to fulfill their dreams are beyond daunting to the average person. They often have a "failure is not an option" attitude that is exceedingly rare yet required for lasting success.

Here's another analogy, and I know that this point has been mentioned before, but it is again relevant. Have you ever had a great idea for an invention? I'm sure you have. Almost everybody has had one or more great ideas for a new product or service. Did you know that great ideas are a dime a dozen? They're everywhere. It's the people who get out there and actually turn an idea into reality that are priceless. So the next time you think, "If only I had thought of that new mousetrap, I'd be rich by now," think again. The idea itself is less than one-tenth of the equation. Action and persistence are the other 90 percent. Bill Gates once said in an interview, "There were a lot of people at the same place I was, and a lot of people had the same vision. The big difference was I took massive and immediate action."

This chapter isn't meant to discourage anyone from advancing to higher positions. It's meant to give you a reality check that can potentially save you from tremendous disappointment and heartache. As always, many of the lessons I describe can be completely learned only through experience. But knowing what's ahead can save you much time and can help you make more informed decisions regarding your future. Often it comes down to who you are and not what you think you want.

"The wise stand out, because they see themselves as part of the whole. They shine, because they don't want to impress. They achieve great things, because they don't look for recognition. Their wisdom is contained in what they are, not their opinions. They refuse to argue, so no one argues with them."

Lao Tzu, Tao Te Ching (5th - 3rd Century BC)

Lesson #6

Code of ethics

Code of ethics

"Life is like a bed of snow. Wherever you walk, your steps will show."

More than seven years in the mortgage business have substantially added to the lessons I've learned. In an industry overrun with characters trying to cut corners to make a quick buck, I sometimes jokingly said that in an industry of lepers, my company was the leper with the most fingers. The mortgage business turned out to be an ideal playground to learn some lessons in ethics.

In the mortgage business you could find dysfunction at all levels. At the top were business owners cheating everyone they could, especially their salespeople. It was very easy for brokers to get rich by not paying their salespeople for whatever lame reasons they could invent. At the bottom were a mass of loan officers, many of whom had some of the worst life habits I'd ever seen.

While the top was motivated by greed, the bottom joined the business as an easy way to make a good living. The mortgage business had a reputation of good money. You also didn't need a degree to work within it — salespeople rarely have one. Most importantly, you didn't need experience. Anyone could get a position as a loan officer.

I believe that a major problem was that people looking to enter the mortgage business confused "good money" with "easy money." Good money doesn't mean it comes easy. It can still involve hard work. Loan officers were looking for easy money, and when they found out that good money and easy money were not the same thing, any semblance of integrity was left at the door. Hard work was simply not part of their equation. Shortcuts were taken on a daily basis, and the only thing that mattered was getting their hands on a commission check. In the process, all problems were blamed on someone else; personal responsibility was an unknown concept to all but a select few professionals. Fraud and forgery proliferated, and rationalization became a way of life for this group of bottom-feeders. Only about 20 percent of loan officers could be considered professionals that you'd enthusiastically refer to friend.

The truth is that unethical people, unethical companies, and unethical business practices can teach us a whole lot about how we can do things better and still thrive in the process.

The proof that what I'm about to tell you is the absolute truth is in my company's survival of the subprime crisis. When the subprime mortgage crisis hit our industry, it caused a virtual meltdown within just a few short months. Liquidity vanished, which meant that lenders couldn't sell their loans to institutional investors and therefore wouldn't or couldn't fund them. To make matters worse, declining property values not only erased homeowners' equity, declining values actually caused tens of thousands of people to owe more on their mortgages than their homes were worth. We called this being upside down.

The industry ground to a virtual halt for almost a year, and hundreds of companies vanished, both lenders and brokers. In fact, some of the largest lenders, such as New Century, went up in flames, sometimes with great scandal. Unethical business practices could be easily found on an institutional level. There were even websites dedicated to tracking the latest implosions.

Within just three months, our volume collapsed by 60 percent of normal as hundreds of loan officers fled the near-impossible new lending guidelines to find salaried employment. Nonetheless, we survived. We were battered, but we survived while other companies disappeared one after another.

I attribute our success to the way we did business. It set us apart from the vast majority of other brokerages in the brokerage industry. I'll describe this to you in the only way that makes sense to me, and that is straightforward and to the point. I'm not trying to portray myself as though I'm sitting on a moral high horse or that I have all the answers. I don't. But I do have some of them.

Our method of doing business was by treating people in the only way I'll allow myself to do business, and that is in a dependable and predictable manner, without cheating anyone. In other words, I treated others the same way I also want to be treated. I always believed that the principle of what goes around comes around is an absolute law of the universe. Conscience aside, I firmly believed that operating ethically would enable us to survive and thrive, and therefore make more money in the long run than by using alternative, less ethical means to make big bucks quickly. My prediction ended up being correct.

Here is my simple secret: In business as in my personal life, I live by a code of ethics that today is the foundation of my being. It guides and rules my actions above all else. Primarily *I live by the agreements that I make.* This defines who I am. I keep my promises and agreements, whatever they may be. It doesn't matter whether it's in writing or not. My word is my bond. This also makes me very predictable when it comes to handling challenges and disputes because anyone simply needs to objectively review the agreement that we made. It will tell them exactly what I'll enforce.

If an agreement needs to be changed, as they sometimes do in business, I don't suddenly enforce the change retroactively or without notice. It has to be win-win, or it will not last. Customers don't bitch; they switch. A long-term and reliable revenue stream is better than a series of quick hits.

There are many aspects to this philosophy, which really shouldn't be anything unusual. Keeping one's agreements should be a given, not an exception. Unfortunately in today's world it's the road less traveled. Maybe it's just the way I'm wired, but I genuinely believe that anyone can benefit from following this advice if they choose to make it their own core value.

I also always show up on time, and I return all my calls within a few hours at most. Whenever possible, I answer my phone so as not to create extra work by shuffling and postponing tasks. I believe that if we postpone something, we create extra work. Furthermore, I believe that if I have to do something, then I might as well do it now. Sooner or later it has to be done anyway. This has made me very efficient, and the result has been that I'm never too busy to do what needs to be done.

As previously mentioned, a fabulously effective trick is to do first what you enjoy the least. That is, start your day in the office with the tasks you don't enjoy so much. Get them out of the way. You'll see that it works wonders to make the rest of the day more pleasant. The alternative is to move through your entire day knowing that some unpleasant tasks still lie ahead. Productivity and our mood will inevitably suffer as we repeatedly postpone those tasks we don't enjoy.

Again, if I have to change an agreement, I do it only if there's no other option. I give advance warning, and I don't impose new regulations or fees on anyone retroactively. My company's simple unique differential was that we were predictable, reliable, and we lived up to our agreements. In the mortgage world it meant that we paid our loan officers on time, every time, and there were no surprises.

I personally paid all commission checks immediately. If someone had to ask me for their money before I got to them, I considered that my personal failure. I do the same with my monthly bills. I always pay bills as they come in. It's not my money, so I don't want it in my bank account. That way I always know how much I have without artificial padding or using other people's money for float or cash flow.

Finally, and possibly most important of all, I take responsibility for my mistakes and rarely have an issue apologizing when warranted. After many years of letting my ego rule my actions, I no longer need to be right. I also don't need to win a negotiation. My preference is to create an agreement that benefits everyone. I believe that creates trust in future dealings. People who find themselves having to walk out of a negotiation feeling like they got the better end of the deal will ultimately suffer unpleasant consequences.

As mentioned already, I believe that what goes around comes around. One of the best explanations of the law of karma I've heard is this: *Whatever you do unto others, good or bad, will be done unto you, but not necessarily by the same person.* This is what some people will never understand. They may get the opportunity to short me, and even if I do not retaliate, someone else will eventually short them. I believe that the law of karma is real because I've experienced it many times. Without fail, I've had to pay for every lapse of judgment in my life. Conversely, I've also reaped the eventual rewards of the good I've done.

The law of karma can also be explained in scientific terms. It is, in essence, Newton's third law. For every action there's an equal and opposite reaction. It's the law of cause and effect. If we understand the law of karma, we can use it to our advantage and thereby influence our future to create more prosperity. It also gives us the right to expect the same courtesies in return from others. I do. I expect the same courtesies from others who deal with me as I grant them. So if you don't do unto me as I do unto you, our interaction will be short-lived.

What I describe has worked to create more prosperity in my life but it also allows me to sleep better at night. I guess I'm driven by my conscience, more so with each passing year.

I've met entirely too many people who have regular ethical lapses, and it always comes back to bite them in the end. Mostly they try to enrich themselves on the backs of others, changing agreements, withholding payment without valid reason, or not repaying loans. Is it any wonder that these same people repeatedly fall on their face no matter what they do? They just don't get it and most never will. These are the same people who are never at fault for anything, who blame everyone except themselves, and who have a desperate need to win. These same individuals are incapable of admitting when they are wrong and are even less capable of apologizing. They have weak egos rather than strong egos. They rarely listen, and they are masters at only one thing — rationalizing their flawed position.

The following is an entertaining true story to illustrate how what goes around eventually comes around.

His name was Fleming, and he was a poor Scottish farmer. One day, while trying to make a living for his family, he heard a cry for help coming from a nearby bog. Fleming dropped his tools and ran to the bog. There, mired to his waist in black muck, was a terrified boy, screaming and struggling to free himself. Farmer Fleming saved the lad from what could have been a slow and terrifying death. The next day, a fancy carriage pulled up to the Scotsman's sparse surroundings. An elegantly dressed nobleman stepped out and introduced himself as the father of the boy Farmer Fleming had saved.

"I want to repay you," said the nobleman. "You saved my son's life."

"No, I can't accept payment for what I did," the Scottish farmer replied, waving off the offer. At that moment, the farmer's own son came to the door.

"Is that your son?" the nobleman asked.

"Yes," the farmer replied proudly.

"I'll make you a deal. Let me provide him with the level of education my own son will enjoy. If the lad is anything like his father, he'll no doubt grow to be a man we both will be proud of." And that he did.

Farmer Fleming's son attended the very best schools and, in time, graduated from St. Mary's Hospital Medical School in London. He went on to become known throughout the world as the noted Sir Alexander Fleming, the discoverer of penicillin.

Years afterward, the same nobleman's son who was saved from the bog was stricken with pneumonia. What saved his life this time? Penicillin. The name of the nobleman? Lord Randolph Churchill. His son's name? Sir Winston Churchill. Someone once said, "What goes around comes around."

This chapter is about integrity. We hear about it a lot, but integrity isn't something that should be talked about a lot. It's about what you do, not what you say. In fact, have you ever met someone who constantly talks about his or her integrity? That person is bad news. I guarantee it. I've learned that this is a sure danger sign and an indication that they probably don't have much integrity. The same goes for a company with the word "Integrity" in their name. Caution! It's like the person who brags and boasts. There's something they're hiding, usually insecurity or unethical behavior in almost all they do. They try to impress us with words, but it usually has the opposite effect. We intuitively know this and shy away from these people. When was the last time a braggart impressed you?

The idea of integrity comes from the Greek concept of *themis*, meaning what's right, and *arête*, meaning excellence for its own sake. Think about it — excellence for its own sake. What a wonderful concept. It's like a charitable donation made anonymously. Integrity is not something you talk about. Integrity is something you do. In fact, integrity is what you do that's right when no one is watching.

A code of ethics, a moral compass, integrity, I believe they are part of a greater formula to lasting success. As part of this formula, an additional ingredient belonging in this chapter is loyalty. Loyalty is a key ingredient that pays never-ending dividends. Most people are constantly on the lookout for vendors who are less expensive, faster, or easier to manipulate. Inevitably they bounce around from vendor to vendor. I believe competition is what drives quality and innovation, but we must not forget that there's always someone cheaper. That doesn't necessarily make them better. So when we repeatedly switch vendors, we are inevitably treated the same way we treat others, as disposable and replaceable individuals of temporary value. What we get in return is a product for our money and nothing more.

Consider that no one becomes successful alone; other people grant us success. Our friends and long-time business acquaintances may bring a new idea to us or offer us a business partnership. Our acquaintances give us jobs or job referrals rather than granting them to a stranger. The vendor we've patronized for years extends us credit as a way of saying thank you when we need it most. Those we have helped, help us.

If you are perceived us a predatory customer who will jump at the first chance to circumvent your vendor when a better deal comes along, what can you expect from that vendor beyond just product? Loyalty creates trust. Trust encourages receiving all that we need to become successful. This includes mentorship and advice, without which we will continue making one expensive mistake after another.

I find it incredibly enlightening and, granted, sometimes satisfying to watch those people who violate the principles of ethics and loyalty over time. They continue to struggle year in and year out waiting for just one more quick hit to springboard them into a better lifestyle. It seems to them that just because they once cheated their way into temporary prosperity, it will work again. Mostly these people live paycheck to paycheck at best and will sell their soul for a buck. Half their time is spent wondering why someone else is successful while they are not. Inevitably they find blame everywhere and with everyone except in the one place that matters, within their own actions. They just don't get it, and most never will.

Let's summarize the major ingredients of living a life of integrity:

- Treat others as you want to be treated. Remember that what goes around comes around. Always.

- Live by your agreements.

- Be honest. It's the foundation to everything else. Without honesty we have nothing.

- Be reliable, punctual, and predictable.

- Create only win-win agreements. Don't try to walk away from the negotiating table feeling like you beat the other side.

- Be loyal to those who treat you right.

- Take responsibility for your mistakes and never hesitate to apologize.

- Pay others before they have a chance to ask you for what you owe them.

- Cultivate your conscience. It will guide you in the right direction.

- Don't talk about integrity. Act with integrity.

Lesson #7

Beware of the person who just went broke!

Beware of the person who just went broke!

It should go without saying that making enemies is not a good idea. Unfortunately, it's almost impossible to completely avoid making enemies as a successful entrepreneur. It's your success that will create some enemies no matter what you do, mostly out of resentment or jealousy, or even resulting from a petty disagreement.

Some people will be envious of your success and hate you for it, even if they show the exact opposite to your face. These are the best friends money can buy, but only so long as you have money. They'd rather see you without it and will use any opportunity to conspire behind your back in order to encourage your demise. There are several reasons for this. Mostly, people do this to feel better about themselves.

Consider this. There are two ways to make yourself appear more successful and thereby elevate your self-esteem and sense of self-worth. One way is to succeed, to become better and do better in life, financially and otherwise. Unfortunately, this is the road less traveled. It takes entirely too much effort for the average person who has little or no self-discipline or life skills. A much simpler way to achieve the same end is to, rather than elevating yourself, depress others around you. If others become less successful, then you, by comparison, appear more successful. This is why even some of your best friends may, consciously or subconsciously, act to harm you. In their world it elevates them. The lower you sink, the higher they appear by comparison, and the better they feel about themselves. If those are your friends, imagine how far a competitor with real vitriol toward you will go to harm you. He won't hesitate one second because your success has severely bruised his earning potential and self-esteem.

Einstein once said, "Great spirits have always encountered violent opposition from mediocre minds." Let's face it: we live in a sea of mediocrity where very few people are ever genuinely happy for you when you succeed because there's nothing in it for them. We are by nature selfish creatures, and human nature includes plenty of undesirable traits such as envy or jealousy. Unfortunately, eliminating mediocre minds from your life is simply not a viable solution because they're everywhere. You simply cannot create a world around yourself that includes only millionaires or successful people. Unsuccessful people, including employees, acquaintances, friends, friends of friends, and sometimes even family members, are everywhere.

There are other factors contributing to man's natural instinct to want to witness your financial funeral. "Misery loves company" is one we can all relate to. How can your unsuccessful friend from high school find solace in his own failures when you're successful and he's not? He can't. He needs someone equally miserable to talk to. If he were smart enough to seek you out as a mentor, he probably wouldn't be so unsuccessful, but that's asking too much of most people. The same applies if he had any real drive and the persistence to succeed no matter what, because that's usually what it takes.

It's so much easier for an unsuccessful person to rationalize your success as the product of luck or having received an unfair advantage somewhere along the line. It allows him to sleep better at night. And if your luck would only change to bring you down to his level, he'd sleep even better. As an added bonus, he'll have his original friend back because he's convinced himself that success has changed you for the worse. Therefore, helping you part with your money will not only serve his purpose, he'll convince himself that he's actually doing you a favor. He'll tell you that money is evil after all. Money can't buy happiness, can't buy health, and so on. Actually, have you ever tried to pay for a medical operation to regain your health without money? Hmm, maybe money *can* buy health after all.

There's a human condition we have no word for in the English language. In German it's called *shadenfroh*. It means taking pleasure in someone else's misfortune for its own sake. Even without selfish gain, real or perceived, we take a perverse pleasure in other people's downfalls. Add *shadenfroh* to the mix, and it's little wonder that anyone manages to keep their wealth with so many piranhas in the water just itching to sink their teeth into you.

Not making enemies is extremely hard when you become successful. Sometimes you'll create enemies merely by some of the tough business decisions that have to be made. You may have to lay someone off who's incompetent or because of forced downsizing. You may win a contract, which also means that someone else lost the contract. An enemy seeking revenge may be the unfortunate result. You may make decisions that others don't like and you may never even find out that you've upset anyone. You may even decide not to hire someone and thereby create an enemy sworn to get revenge on you because he or she took it personally or felt they were discriminated against. There are many ways of inadvertently creating enemies, even if you are the nicest person in the world.

As a successful individual, you have a responsibility to minimize the enemies you create by being sensitive to the effect your actions have on other people. You'll never be able to completely eliminate your impact on individuals who are prone to resentment, envy, or revenge for an imagined slight you caused them. However, you should be particularly cautious of one group of individuals, and that is the primary purpose of this chapter. They can be immensely damaging, and they can be truly dangerous.

These individuals will waste your time and cost you unnecessary money to clean up the mess they often create. These are individuals who just went broke. An example might be a paycheck-to-paycheck employee who has been laid off. Without a new source of income to replace the old, they need someone to blame for their misfortune. You, of course, make a great target. If someone just went broke, it's important to remember that they have nothing to lose and you have everything to lose. They know this also. They may be so low on the ladder of life that you've given them a real purpose in life to get even with you for the smallest wrong you may have caused them, real or imagined.

Your dispute with such an individual may be over only $100, such as a commission they didn't earn but think they're entitled to. No matter how right you may be, convincing them of that is a whole different matter. Remember, simple minds always think they're right.

A fully justified "no" over a matter of a few dollars may cause you a nightmare in headaches and legal fees. Often they'll strike at you by tapping into free government services or legal representation on contingency, no matter how cumbersome the process may be for them. Standing in line for hours on end and wading through endless bureaucracy and letter writing won't deter them. In fact, this becomes their new occupation. They have nothing else to do, and you've become the symbol for all that's wrong with the world and their life.

What makes this lesson even harder to deal with is that you're at another disadvantage. They're the underdog and therefore have sympathy on their side. Every bureaucrat they talk to who has an ax to grind with their own boss suddenly becomes your guy's best friend. As I said before, misery loves company.

In liberal states such as California, the problem is multiplied. California is extremely unfriendly to employers. It doesn't matter who's right; the employer is automatically considered guilty unless proven innocent, and even then the costs can be horrendous.

Can you tell that this was a tough lesson for me to learn? I truly wish I had known about this fifteen or twenty years ago. I don't mean to imply that you should cave in to every nutcase who wants to extort you for a hundred bucks. That's not the lesson. The lesson is in knowing the potential consequences of standing on principle or insisting that you're right even when you really are right. Think about your actions and don't get into a spitting contest over little to nothing. It may not be worth the price. A wonderful saying I often refer to is, "You can be right or you can be happy, but you cannot be both." It applies especially to relationships, but if you think about it, you'll see that it applies to business also.

The easiest way to recognize that you may have a potential problem such as what I'm describing is when someone thinks you owe them money when you know you don't. All the documentation in the world may not convince them that they weren't owed a commission or whatever grievance they think they have. The problem is that this may be money they're counting on to pay bills.

I once had someone call me two years after they worked for me to try to convince me that I owed him $150 dollars. Needless to say, they just went broke and needed money. My biggest fright came about fifteen years ago when an employee left my company thinking I still owed him $80. He tried to get even with me by writing to every government agency he could think of to try to cause me trouble. Fortunately, his scheme didn't work since most government agencies are used to hearing from disgruntled employees who have been terminated. But it caused me one heck of a scare when I found out.

I've stood in court with terminated employees suing me who had such outlandish claims and stories that the judge just shook his head. Watch any TV courtroom reality show and you'll see how blind someone can be in regards to their own perceived grievance and how they'll rationalize their claim to the ends of the earth. Don't forget that once they start, they cannot stop, even if eventually they do recognize at some point that they were wrong. People typically cannot admit they are wrong and will fight to the death to prove themselves right. No wonder a cynical yet wise man once said (I think it was me), "I love humanity. I just don't like all humans."

If you have salespeople or customers who feel they've been shorted, consider that you may lose them to the competition over a few dollars. Is it worth it in the long run? This can be an expensive mistake for the satisfaction of being right. Again, I'm not advocating necessarily giving in to everyone. How you deal with the conflict is most important.

Being aware of your potential loss ahead of time is your best strategy as it will guide your actions to be more diplomatic. If it's in your long-term self-interest to give in, then sometimes that may be the right thing to do. Just be careful that you don't set a precedent that will repeat itself. Once word gets out that you compromised, everyone will be at your door wanting the same thing. Having a firm, detailed set of guidelines where everyone knows the rules ahead of time has always worked best for me.

If things get unpleasant with such a character as I described and the situation requires you to stand on principle as every good businessman has to at times, be prepared to strike back if that person doesn't back down. Go in with all guns blazing and be willing to stay the course, but don't bluff or make threats you can't back up. In fact, wealthy people should have a reserve fund for such eventualities. A past mentor of mine referred to it as "F U Money." If someone tries to extort you, use it to sue them, strike back, or whatever you need to do within legal limits to get them to back off. Don't count this money in your assets. Consider it already spent. Sooner or later you'll have to spend it anyway. It's a last resort, but sometimes it's the only way out.

As maturity and experience in business eventually made me a better businessman, I also spent countless hours trying to figure out the root of the problem with people who are failures and whose life skills are so deplorable that you need to watch out for them. It occupies my mind because I am by nature a teacher who wants to help people learn how to help themselves.

How do you motivate someone? How do you help someone develop better habits? How can you get someone to apply the correct solutions to their repeated mistakes even when they wholeheartedly agree that your advice is the solution to their problems? How can you save people from destroying themselves? The truth is you can't, even when they agree with you and acknowledge with the utmost sincerity that the guidance you described is the right advice. They have to want it themselves. They have to want it so badly that they'll make the necessary changes in their habits and behavior. And that, no one can give them. It can only come from within.

Johns Hopkins foreign affairs professor Michael Mandelbaum once said, "People don't change when you tell them there is a better option. They change when they conclude that they have no other option." Maybe I've become cynical, but in my experience even that is optimistic. Nonetheless, all you can do is offer guidance. As they say, when the student is ready, the teacher will appear. You can be that teacher, but if the student isn't ready, you can be the Dalai Lama and it won't mean a thing.

The question remains. What causes someone to strike out at you even when it's obvious they're wrong? When you realize the answer, a whole lot of things may fall into place for you as this revelation did for me. It comes down to one thing, humiliation. People who fail feel humiliated. Anger and frustration are the results, then hopelessness, and then they lash out.

Going broke is humiliating. Failure is humiliating. Seeing other people rise above you while you continue to struggle is humiliating. It doesn't matter that it may be your own fault. Sometimes it is and sometimes it isn't. The feeling of humiliation remains the same. More than anything else, being proven wrong is humiliating.

When someone feels humiliated, they lash out — at society or at you. This is in large part why we have Islamic terrorism in the world. The root is the humiliation Muslims feel for being left out of the growth of global prosperity and opportunity, without even a voice in their future. Although their regimes make billions in oil revenues, little trickles down to the people. When all Arab countries combined filed as many international patents in a twenty-year period (171 between 1980 and 1999) as Hewlett Packard files about every two weeks (or about 11 per day), then it's painfully obvious how Muslims are being left behind. Millions of Chinese people now have hope they never had before, as do increasing numbers of Indian people. But Muslims still have little or no hope and are literally being excluded. Where there is no hope, there is humiliation. Where there is humiliation, there is a need for someone to blame. The West is it. 9/11 was an attempt to humiliate us in return.

Even Nazi Fascism grew out of the humiliation and loss of dignity Germany felt after World War I. The Treaty of Versailles required Germany to pay reparations for the damage it did, something it could ill afford after the total devastation it suffered. The result was a national attempt at getting even with the rest of the world. On a personal level, it can be speculated that Hitler's motivation was actually rooted in an attempt to get even with all the people who had rejected him as an artist. Pure and simple, Hitler was humiliated when his art was not appreciated.

Humiliation is an expression of ego, and you should never underestimate the ability of the ego to destroy that which it most seeks to protect. When our ego seeks to protect the self, it engages in various protective measures, such as becoming overly defensive, all of which, without fail, do more harm than good to its host. In essence, the ego blindly contributes to its own destruction. In similar fashion, Muslims lash out at the only potential savior from their oppressive regimes, American-style freedom.

Remember, disputes happen, and enemies can come out of the most unlikely places for any number of reasons. They're a part of doing business, and you can never avoid them entirely. But the one adversary you particularly want to watch out for is the guy or gal who just went broke. He or she feels humiliated and needs someone to blame ... and now you're it. They've got nothing to lose, and you have everything to lose. Beware and watch out for them. Think before you act. You'll be glad you did.

Lesson #8

Traits of success

Traits of success

Why do some people find it easier to achieve success than others? In fact, why is it almost impossible for some people to become successful no matter what they do? The reason some people find it so much easier to achieve success is that they are predisposed for success as a result of their core philosophy of life and also from the habits that develop as the result of their philosophy and unique character traits. Individuals who have the opposite philosophy and character traits are typically doomed to remain failures.

Fortunately, the character traits I'm referring to can be developed and cultivated. Success can be attained by each and every one of us if we understand what's keeping us from becoming successful.

By examining a person's habits and core beliefs, you can predict their probability of success if they decide to pursue a better life. You can even use this to predict your own chances if you are willing to be 100 percent objective. The caveat in this is that your philosophy and habits cross over into political territory. That is, conservative thinkers have a different disposition toward success than liberal thinkers.

If you are on the wrong side of the aisle, you may not agree with me simply because of your core convictions. If you have a dependency mentality or you believe that all wealthy people acquired their prosperity through dishonest means, then you're at a disadvantage and your chances for success are dramatically reduced. Truthfully, that's a problem only you can deal with. Nonetheless, I sincerely hope that you'll examine the issue in minute detail and make the appropriate adjustments. If you don't, I can't change that. No one will be able to help you except yourself.

The information I'm about to provide you is proven and is the result of countless studies examining the habits of successful people versus those who continue to struggle endlessly.

For me, this information was a revelation as I've spent countless hours tutoring people on how to move their lives forward. It took me a long time to figure out why some people simply continued to fail no matter how hard I or they tried. I was banging my head against the wall in frustration. I wanted to help. What was I doing wrong? The truth was that I wasn't doing anything wrong. It was their underlying foundation and belief system that was simply not conducive to achieving wealth and success. I couldn't help them if they were unwilling to adjust their beliefs and resulting habits no matter how hard I tried.

Once I figured this out, a great weight was lifted from my shoulders. Additionally, this information became very valuable in understanding what kind of a business relationship was possible with a particular person and to what degree my mentoring them on the principles of success had the potential to have a positive impact on their lives.

The key difference between people is in the area of personal responsibility and independence versus a dependency and entitlement mentality. People who take responsibility for every aspect of their lives and who do not blame others, including family, for unfortunate events in their past, were much more open to making mistakes, recognizing their mistakes, and to keep trying until they succeeded. The rest were too busy with regret and resentment to open their eyes to the vast possibilities surrounding them. These were often also the same people who frowned upon success, believing that successful people made their money as a result of cheating, inheritance, or dumb luck. Nothing could be further from the truth as the majority of successful people are self-made, hardworking, and honest. In fact, it has been said that money makes a good man better and a bad man worse. The best of men are made humble by money.

Here are some of the ingredients that become the foundation of a person's predisposition for success. These ingredients can be cultivated so that you too can become successful.

The first ingredient you'll find in a successful person is gratitude. They are thankful for everything they have in life, even if it's not much. Unsuccessful people feel they are owed something, and they carry resentment with them wherever they go. They blame others for their failures, whereas the successful person will always take responsibility for his or her missteps and past misfortunes so that he can learn from the experience and not repeat the same mistake twice. In line with this is that successful people want others to succeed also. Unsuccessful people want others to fail because misery loves company. If someone else fails, then it makes them feel better in comparison.

Another key feature that stands out in unsuccessful people is that they think they know it all and will defend their viewpoints to their death. A sad commentary on their lives is that the more they claim to always know it all, the less they actually know. They do not know all the things that they do not know, and rarely if ever do they have the motivation to change that.

If you've ever listened to a world-renowned scientist like Albert Einstein, they invariably all say the same thing. The more they learn, the more they realize they have left to learn. The many wonders of the universe have made them humble in their genius. Unsuccessful people are often know-it-alls, and this demonstrates only how ignorant they really are.

Einstein was once asked how it feels to be the most brilliant person in the world. He replied something along the lines of, "I don't know. You should go ask Nicola Tesla."

A deeper understanding of what we know and do not know is helpful for further introspection. According to Kevin Trudeau, there are four levels of knowledge, or lack thereof. Sometimes we move from one to another as if they are phases we must go through. I find the first two most relevant to this discussion. They are:

- Unconscious ignorance – when you don't know that you don't know

- Conscious ignorance – when you know that you don't know

- Conscious competence – when you know that you know but you have to make a conscious effort to bring forth what you know in order to use it

- Unconscious competence – when using your knowledge becomes second nature. The information is fully internalized and a part of you

Another observation concerning successful individuals is that every leader is a reader. All successful people read and are lifelong learners. But they also read the right material. It has been said that if you want to become rich, then stop reading what poor people read. Find out what successful people recommend and read that.

Classical scholar Desiderius Erasmus said, "When I get a little money, I buy books, and if any is left, I buy food and clothes."

You simply *cannot* succeed if you do not read good books, especially motivational and inspirational self-help material.

Successful people use multiple to-do lists, and they set regular goals, both short term and long term. They are never without goals. Some may even keep a journal. How many unsuccessful people do you know who use to-do lists other than grocery lists and who set regular goals? Not many, I'm sure.

Successful people compliment and forgive others. They also embrace change. Unsuccessful people criticize and hold a grudge against others and are apprehensive of change.

Do you see the differences in people's core values, their character, habits, and underlying belief system? It matters enormously, not just for a predisposition toward success, but also for your happiness. Successful people display a joy of life, whereas unsuccessful people are typically internally angry.

Remember that success is not just about money. Success is about achievement, productivity, contribution, and fulfillment in all aspects of your life. The money just follows.

Our attitude is a choice we all make, for better or for worse. But know that if you are angry inside, you can change it. As they say, if you force yourself to smile long enough, eventually you'll stop frowning. It's true. You can fake it until you make it. Try it. Force yourself to be positive for an entire day and then notice that it will become easier the next day, and so on. Keep it up until *it becomes a part of you, and you'll change your life. Happiness and a positive attitude are habits that can be cultivated, regardless of your circumstances.*

Finally, successful people think in positive terms, and unsuccessful people think in negative terms. "I can" versus "I can't." The glass is half-full versus half-empty. There have been more books written on this one self-help topic than any other. What you think and how you think is what you'll become. We create the reality around us with our thoughts.

God made us to be co-creators. Your current life is a compilation of your past thoughts. Change your thoughts, and you change your life. I recommend you pick up any of the following books as the scope of this information is too broad for inclusion in this text. Choose from among *Think and Grow Rich* by Napoleon Hill, *The Strangest Secret* by Earl Nightingale, *As Man Thinketh* by James Allen, *As You Think, So Shall You Become* also by James Allen, and most recently *The Secret* by Rhonda Byrne. There are many more. You can literally think your way into a more fulfilling life. In fact, it's the only way. Read one or more of these books, and your life will never again be the same. I guarantee it.

I know a wonderful gentleman named Ron Heagy who is now in his fifties. One day before turning eighteen years old, he had a surfing accident that landed him in a wheelchair as he became paralyzed from the neck down. He has been unable to walk or move for over thirty years.

Ron is one of the most positive individuals I've ever met. He has given numerous inspirational speeches on the effect your attitude has on your life, and he is a living example of this. He's happy, married to a wonderful woman named Kelli, a father, and I've never seen him express any kind of negativity or resentment. He managed to get a master's degree and became an accomplished mouth painter. He even created a nonprofit camp for handicapped children named Camp Attitude. His accomplishments speak volumes about what your beliefs and your attitude are capable of accomplishing. If being a quadriplegic has not kept Ron from achieving happiness and fulfillment, shouldn't you be able to do the same?

In summary, people are either predisposed for success or for failure. This predisposition comes from your core values, attitude, and beliefs. These beliefs determine how you view the world and success. Your view develops your habits, and your habits determine whether you'll succeed or not.

No one is born with perfect attitude, beliefs, values, and habits. But everyone can cultivate them and thereafter achieve whatever heights of greatness they desire. That includes you.

Lesson #9

Motivation, it's like food and water!

Motivation, it's like food and water!

Have you ever been to a Tony Robbins seminar or any other type of motivational seminar? They can be incredibly inspiring, effective, and tons of fun. I highly recommend listening to motivational speakers. No matter how many you've seen or been to, there's always something new and useful to learn. Every successful person listens to personal-development information. Even motivational speakers listen to other motivational speakers on a regular basis, not to see what the competition is up to, but to keep themselves inspired.

As I've attended and taught at multiple seminars, I've watched so many wonderful people come alive with hope and energy, planning for and dreaming of a better future. They're literally glowing, and they finish the seminar fully amped with enthusiasm. That's the promise of a good motivational seminar, and it typically delivers 100 percent every time.

Personal-development seminar attendees learn exactly what to do by the time the lecture is over and can't wait to get home to put their new life on a never-ending trajectory toward success. And then saddest thing happens to entirely too many of them. Two to three weeks after the seminar is over, their life is exactly where it was before the seminar with no change and no forward momentum. Their day-to-day routine is exactly what it used to be, and when asked what happened, they don't know. "Life happens," is the most common explanation.

Well, I know what really happened.

A personal-growth or success seminar is designed to motivate you and provide you with information and tools to transform your life. And this it does incredibly well. The problem is that one key piece of information is always left out of its message. And that is that motivation is like food and water. You need to replenish it on a daily basis. The moment you stop feeding yourself with motivational or personal-growth information, it all fades away.

It's exactly like eating and drinking. You cannot just eat once and hope that your stomach will remain full. It obviously doesn't. Motivation is the same. You need to feed yourself regularly and consistently. This doesn't mean you have to go to a motivational seminar every two weeks. But it does mean that to keep your momentum going, you need to read self-help books, watch DVDs, and listen to audio recordings. And you need to do it virtually every day of your life. Fortunately, good material is enjoyable, and it elevates your mood in the process. So don't think it's a chore that you won't like. If it makes you feel good, you'll look forward to it.

An even better analogy is going to the gym. If you work out every day for an entire week, you can achieve some noticeable results. But can you then stop and hope that your muscles remain in their new and improved state? No, of course not. You need to keep going to the gym on a regular basis. It's the same with personal growth, success, and motivational material. You need to keep yourself immersed in it, ideally forever.

Motivational, self-help, or personal-development information is available to anyone who seeks it. There are countless seminars, books, videos, and audio recording to choose from. You should tap into all of them. They contain down-to-earth, real information that can be applied for a positive outcome immediately. The results and transformation they're capable of achieving in your life are nothing short of miraculous, but only if you keep the momentum going with ongoing studies. Even listening to books on tape in your car is transformative and one of the easiest ways to keep yourself immersed.

Your life will never be the same if you keep it up. The information, by its very nature, is positive. As mentioned, this has the added benefit of elevating your mood. It gives your future hope and promise, and then delivers real results.

There are three kinds of people in the world. There are those who ignore personal-growth information or don't even know it exists and how transformative it can be. Those are the masses, over 90 percent of all people. Then there are those who will go to a seminar for example, but then think that this is enough to propel their lives toward success. These people are definitely in the minority. But the smallest segment of the population is the third type of person, the rare individual who understands the information in this chapter and envelops their entire being in ongoing personal-development information. Those individuals succeed in ways that even they could have never fathomed prior to their transformation. I want you to become one of those individuals.

Here's a quick story from my life to illustrate my point: I've been a student of the aforementioned information almost all my life. It's propelled me to repeated and ever-increasing heights of success. It's become such an integral part of my being that even if I take a break, the lessons never completely disappear from within me. But this doesn't mean I can permanently remove myself — as I found out the hard way.

Six years ago my wife gave birth to our baby boy, Gabriel. He's the light of my life and a gift from God unlike any other. Needless to say, my life changed as my priorities changed. Life became filled with distractions as our son became our priority. The type of books I read changed, and the limitation on my ability to travel also limited my ability to visit personal-development seminars. The bottom line is that I almost stopped immersing myself in success-oriented information. During this time I still built a spectacularly successful company, but in retrospect I know I felt that something was missing.

One day, while my business partner, Steve, and I were on an airplane to visit our stores in Hawaii, I noticed that he was reading a book on business lessons by Richard Branson called *Like A Virgin*. Something clicked inside me, and I requested to have a look at his book. My adrenaline immediately spiked as I realized I hadn't read personal-growth material in far too long. I committed to go buy the same book as soon as we landed and did so without hesitation.

I read the entire book within two days, and my being came alive as I realized that I had lost my way. I had lost who I really was. It wasn't the specific information I was reading but the sense that I had been missing out.

From that day forward, I started reading and listening to the right type of material again, the type of material that I had cherished for my entire adult life. Immediately things began to change. Wonderful coincidences reappeared and multiplied. The universe started to again respond to all my requests and desires. If you are wondering what I mean by that, the second half of the chapter on goal setting and the last chapter on destiny will illustrate my point. Nonetheless, here's an example: I had recently sold my business, and in my mind I thought that whatever I did next, I wanted it to include public speaking as I love to be on stage. Within two weeks I was asked to do a lecture. I asked and I received.

The point is this: If you're in the right frame of mind and know the technique, whenever you ask the universe for something, as long as it's positive, the universe will answer and provide. It's a universal law.

This experience brought me back on track. I felt like myself again, and I felt much more fulfilled. I was back!

This book will fulfill its promise of teaching you lessons that will help you to become successful in less time and for less money and with fewer mistakes than what you could expect without it. But this does not mean you should stop there. You need to immerse yourself in ongoing personal-growth information from seminars, more books, video presentations, and audio recordings. Motivation is literally like food and water. You need it every day to truly thrive.

Lesson #10

Finding a mentor

Finding a mentor

If there's a technique for achieving success that stands taller than any other, that is finding a mentor to teach you what he knows.

Napoleon Hill once said, "The surest, fastest way to wealth is to follow in the footsteps of someone who has already done it."

Lessons such as the ones found in this book and many more can be acquired from someone who has become a self-made success story over a long, diverse entrepreneurial career. Choose someone who is already successful so that the lessons they share with you come from experience and not from theory or wishful thinking. Remember, you don't learn to parachute from someone who hasn't successfully jumped out of an airplane at least 500 times and lived to tell about it. Likewise, you don't learn how to get rich from a poor person.

Ideally you'll choose someone who has experienced some hardships and at least one major failure in their business life. The most important life-transforming lessons don't come from our successes. They come from our failures. I'm referring to the type of failure that appears to be an all-consuming dead end where only the resilience and persistence of one of those rare individuals who can overcome virtually any setback got them past their disaster. Do not deny yourself the wisdom that can come from someone who has lost virtually everything and then rebounded to even greater heights of prosperity.

The technique for finding a mentor to guide you and learn from is surprisingly simple. This technique can also be applied for getting almost anything else you may want help with.

The secret is to appeal to someone's sense of willingness to help. This works especially well with successful people because almost every self-made success story feels deep gratitude for the gifts life has given them and therefore has a strong desire to give back. A special select few even recognize that among those gifts are their failures.

Successful people want to help other people become successful. They want to teach their techniques and secrets because it's a way of giving back for the abundance they have been granted in life.

The wording you use when asking for mentorship is key. Use something along the lines of, "I admire what you've accomplished in life. I'd like to learn how to become successful also and I'm willing to do whatever it takes. Would you be willing to teach me how you've become successful and be my mentor?"

Such wording can be used equally with a multimillionaire or with a receptionist whose help you need to get through to the top person on the phone.

If you are making a sales call and need to get past the call screener, be polite and *ask for help*. Everybody loves to feel that they are being appreciated for the help they provide. Try something along the lines of, "I could really use your help. I'd like an audience with the person who makes decisions regarding your advertising. Would you be so kind as to let me know who that is and help me get to talk to that person? I would really appreciate your help." Doesn't that sound a whole lot more effective than, "Hello, who handles your advertising?"

When it comes to mentoring, a regret many successful people have is that they often don't have someone to mentor. Most people feel that successful people are unapproachable, and therefore they never ask. But successful people want to give back. They want to feel appreciated, and most will jump at the opportunity to give back. You can use this to your advantage, and in the process you're also giving something very valuable to your new mentor, the ability to help someone do what they've done to become prosperous.

One final note: It doesn't really matter what field you're looking to dive into. Your potential mentor does not need to be in the same field although it may be a bonus if he is. Business skills are transferrable. A good businessman or entrepreneur can thrive in almost any field. The most important skills are general business skills, like management skills. These aren't specific to any one industry. A good manager can manage in the telecommunications industry just as well as in the automotive industry.

Look for someone who loves what they're doing. My number one criteria is always to enter a field that looks really, really interesting to me. If I'm passionate about what I'm doing, then I automatically look forward to going to work each day. In fact, if I love what I do, then it's not work to me. Money is never a primary criterion for me, and it shouldn't be for you either. If you do something you are passionate about, you'll be good at it, and the money will automatically follow. It's the enthusiasm for the work your new mentor does that will make his mentorship that much more enjoyable for both sides.

Finding a mentor is invaluable to your trajectory toward success. Mentors aren't difficult to find as successful people want to give back. Appeal to their sense of willingness to help a less experienced person and enjoy the ride. You may make a new friend in the process who will introduce you to more successful people.

Lesson #11

Stay on trend

Stay on trend

Every time I move from one business to another, I go through a period of nothingness where my previous business has been closed and I don't yet know what I'm going to do next. This lull period used to scare me as I was afraid I wouldn't find something new before my money ran out. I'm no longer afraid — not because I'm now financially secure, but because I know the exact pattern to expect. In essence, I have full confidence in myself that I'll come up with my next great business. The only thing that still causes me some anxiety is not having enough to do during this period of transition. I actually enjoy going to work every morning as I'm always working in an industry I love. So my only challenge is to find something new that I'll love as much or more than my previous venture without going through a long period of inactivity.

In reviewing the businesses I've started throughout my career, I noticed that the most successful ones rode a trend that lasted at least a few years before dying out. This isn't for everyone because of the emotional ups and downs that accompanies this type of rollercoaster career. Nonetheless, there are some important lessons to be learned here that can benefit you.

One of the lessons I learned was to trust myself to find something new. As they say, when the going gets tough, the tough get going. I'm definitely in that category. When I'm up against a wall, whether it's a business challenge in my existing business or even finding a new business, my internal resources mobilize. Most people give up. I come alive. Using the goal-setting techniques I described in a previous chapter, I put it out to the universe that I expect to find something new. This technique has never failed me. I talk to people, and I become very observant as I look for any clue to something interesting.

The ideas that I turn into reality are not always my own, but a talent that should be easy for anyone to cultivate is to recognize a good idea wherever it comes from. It may be something someone says that sparks an idea, or it may be something in the marketplace where someone else is breaking new ground. All good ideas and new trends develop competitors, so there's no reason you cannot follow what someone else is successfully doing for the first time. Some of my original ideas have been copied by others as well. I consider it a compliment. Imitation really is the best form of flattery.

I have numerous examples of new businesses I started where I entered into them near the beginning of a trend. I definitely rode a wave in the mortgage business for about seven years. It came to a screeching halt when the subprime crisis hit. My favorite trend was the gold and diamond buying business. It started with a Super bowl commercial by the founding company of the industry, and then it lasted for five years for me. I entered the business about a year after it started and exited when gold prices dropped too far to maintain adequate margins. We, along with our major competitors, had also taken so much gold out of the marketplace that most people didn't have much left to sell. The business will never disappear entirely, but until gold prices jump back to normal levels, I'll remain on the sidelines.

The point is that there's always a new wave to ride. If you find one, make sure it's something you'd love to be involved in — not for the money, but for the joy and fulfillment it will bring you. It should also be something where you do something worthwhile, something where your product or service helps other people.

Trends are extremely lucrative in that a rising tide will lift all ships. That is, if you have the required general business skills, it's easier to become successful in something that's on trend. In German there's a word for this, *zeitgeist*. It means sign of the times.

Here's a trick that will help you find the next trend: Motivational speaker T. Harv Ecker also refers to this technique as the easiest way to get rich in America today. It's very simple. Find something that works in one area that hasn't yet made it everywhere and duplicate it where it doesn't yet have a presence. The quintessential example is Starbucks. Franchised coffee shops started in the northwestern United States and have since spread to every corner of the globe. If you'd visited Seattle when Starbucks was starting out and took the concept to somewhere else like southern California, where coffee shops were not yet on every street corner, you would have had an opportunity for riches beyond comprehension. You could have opened your own chain of coffee shops or even become a Starbucks franchisee.

Using this technique of finding a new trend may involve some travel — travel to a neighboring county or state, or even a different country. If you visit Italy, for example, you'll find businesses there that do not even exist over here. You'll also find businesses that exist here but not there. Or you may find businesses that exist here and there but with a different twist. Either offers opportunity. You could test a popular concept from there in your own neighborhood, or you could do the opposite: take something that's working well in your neighborhood and try it elsewhere.

The power in a trend is momentum. People talk about it. It's new and exciting. The momentum created by those who started the trend will help carry forward the newer entries into the marketplace and make success for them that much easier.

Creating a trend yourself is also a possibility. I've done it several times, but it's sometimes paved with danger. My first business ever, a fast-food delivery service, apparently created a trend of imitators in southern California. However, other than my lack of business experience at that time holding me back, the concept took a while to penetrate the imagination of the general public. Hence, my company never made much money. Followers to the trend I created did much better as they had momentum on their side.

Another danger with creating a new trend is that you may be treading in previously uncharted legal territory. Often the founder of a trend gets clobbered with new laws that get enacted as a result of his new type of business. If a new industry has no regulation yet, you can bet that it won't be long before regulators seize the opportunity to do what they like doing best. Imitators and followers reap the benefits as they step into territory that now has a firm set of guidelines. This has happened to me, and it was indescribably painful. You can read the description of this event in the final chapter on destiny.

Always try to stay on trend. Trends have momentum, thereby increasing your chances for rapid success. Look ahead and don't go where the industry is; go where it's going. Wayne Gretzky once said, *"Most hockey players skate to where the puck is. I try to skate to where it's going."*

Lesson #12

Security

Security

Many people ask themselves whether the quest for success is worth it. Once they learn that success is not about what you're going to get but what you're willing to give up to get it, then a lot of people will start wondering whether leaving their perceived security is worth it. After all, they have a guaranteed paycheck every two weeks, paid vacation, decent job security, and worry-free weekends to look forward to. Why take the plunge into unknown territory if there's no guarantee of success?

Although some successful people are driven in a way that gives them no choice as to what type of life to pursue (I am one of them), others take a conscious plunge into the unknown despite all the comforts and security of the nine-to-five existence they leave behind. But is the middle-class nine-to-five lifestyle really secure? Are entrepreneurs really risk takers who put it all on the line? Even when they succeed, don't they still live with the fear that they could lose it all again and suddenly find themselves broke and unemployed?

Let's examine both choices side by side. I'm going to make one assumption, and it's relevant to the entrepreneur: an entrepreneur will do whatever it takes to learn the business skills required to run a company and be an effective manager — that is, if they don't know them already. I'm referring to the business skills that are transferrable to practically any business. As I mentioned before, a good businessman has skills that are not unique to any one industry. They are portable from one business to almost any other. With that in mind, who has security and who is the risk taker?

As a nine-to-five employee, do you own your job, or can someone take it away from you? You can obviously be fired at any time without warning, so the job is yours only for as long as your boss allows it to be yours.

Can you give yourself a raise? Well, you can work harder to try to earn yourself a raise, but under whose control is it ultimately? It's under your boss's control.

Do you have the right to work whatever hours you want? No, of course not. You're required to work a certain number of hours, and you are required to work during the specified hours that the business is open.

Do you have the right to take a vacation any time you want? Not really. You also cannot take as much vacation as you'd like. You have to follow your company's rules and policies.

As an employee, you are also subject to the ups and downs of your industry and the economy as a whole. But it doesn't stop there. Employees have virtually no control over how much they pay in taxes as available deductions for salaried employees are very limited. Your retirement is also not under your control. Someone else controls when you should retire and even if you should retire. There are people like myself who love to work and never want to retire. The thought of someone else telling me it's over is simply frightening.

Here's the world of the entrepreneur:

At first, as an entrepreneur you'll work more than what you get paid for. This is where discipline comes into the picture. Discipline is being able to postpone short-term gratification in favor of longer-term benefits. This is what entrepreneurs do; they look to the future. Their long-term goals are more important than short-term gratification. You see, once your business is up and running, growing and thriving, you'll get paid for much more than the time your work would typically justify. At first, your hourly income is pitifully low, but once you arrive, your hourly income will be much higher than most employees could ever earn. In some cases an entrepreneur's income will reach stratospheric heights. So let's see who's in control.

The entrepreneur ultimately controls his own income, when he gets paid, and how much he gets paid. When and how much vacation he takes is also his choice.

Who makes the rules that have to be followed? The entrepreneur makes his own rules and company policies, obviously within legal guidelines. He also cannot be fired. But what if the business ultimately fails? Many do. Remember our assumption that the entrepreneur has taught himself transferrable skills. He can simply open a new business in any field he desires. And because of his superior financial position, he should have more than enough savings to survive the time between businesses.

So who has more security, the nine-to-five employee or the entrepreneur? Clearly, the entrepreneur does. He controls his own destiny because he created it. It's his to do with as he pleases. Whether it fails or succeeds is also under the entrepreneur's control.

Entrepreneurs are not always the all-or-nothing risk takers that people believe them to be. Entrepreneurs take risks, yes, but smart entrepreneurs take only calculated risks and always have a backup plan in case something doesn't work out. They rarely put everything on the line even if they are frequently faced with roadblocks that seem insurmountable. For someone with a truly entrepreneurial spirit and personality, failure is not an option. And it's precisely that attitude that will ultimately guarantee him or her success.

An entrepreneur is also not a slave to the ups and down of the economy, their industry, or anything else. They can move on, do it again, or do something else. In fact, downturns in the economy are when many entrepreneurs shine. They find opportunities and needs that can be filled, and often they have learned to capitalize on cycles and trends. It's definitely not rare for entrepreneurs to thrive during bad times.

It's been said that fortunes aren't made during good times; they're made during bad times. You only collect during the good times. This means that when the economy turns south, prices often tumble, businesses are up for sale, and the entire country basically becomes one big yard sale. A savvy entrepreneur will go shopping for opportunities that will turn to gold when things turn around. Seeds are sowed and nurtured during the bad times. They blossom during the good times.

So who has more security? In my opinion, it's obviously the entrepreneur as he's learned one thing beyond all else. He's learned to create and control his own destiny. He provides himself with security by virtue of his skills. In so many ways, he is truly his own boss and the master of his fate. As I mentioned in the chapter on goal setting, the best way to predict your future is to create it.

Lesson #13

Break the rules, not the law

Break the rules, not the law

An entrepreneur's success is often the result of their creativity and ability to think outside the box. What they do is different. What they create is different. How they create things is different. They break many of the rules that are considered conventional wisdom on how to do things. That's their genius. But breaking the rules is not the same as breaking the law. Breaking the rules can make you rich, whereas breaking the law can get you into deep trouble.

It's important to discuss the law in this text because very few entrepreneurs intentionally break the law. However, a surprising number eventually do, albeit sometimes without realistically being able to avoid it or ever intending to. Hence, I want to discuss this and provide you with some insight on how to stay on the right side of the law.

Although America is still considered to be the land of opportunity and the easiest place in the world for an entrepreneur to realize their dreams, our system of laws and regulations is becoming increasingly stacked against the small business owner. There are a number of reasons for this. The most obvious is that for many regulations there's a fee associated with complying with that regulation. Regulations are a source of government revenue.

Often the requirement is to get a license, and there's always a cost associated with obtaining a license. Many of these are ridiculous, unnecessary intrusions into our lives and nothing but an indirect tax. I've received bills from government agencies that never had any interaction with my business except to send me an annual bill.

Much of the system is broken. There's simply no other way to say it. Outside of unnecessary regulation, laws and regulations can be the result of sincere efforts by regulators to provide guidelines within which we must operate so as to operate in a fair, competitive environment. The problem is that too many people are engaged in being professional do-gooders so that the number of regulations we eventually face becomes nothing short of unmanageable.

Then there's a more sinister reason for the excessive plethora of laws and regulations, to the point where many of them contradict each other. That is, by abiding by one law you may be violating another. Laws may also be so difficult to interpret that even lawmakers cannot agree on the correct interpretation. The IRS rule book is a perfect example, all 75,000 pages! Nonetheless, we're told that ignorance of the law is not an excuse, and no matter how hard a law is to interpret, we'll always lose that day in court.

The easiest way to explain this unfortunate reality is from an excerpt from one of the best books ever written, *Atlas Shrugged* by Ayn Rand. It is generally accepted that Atlas Shrugged is considered the second-most influential book in this country, second only to the Bible. Here's the passage.

"Did you really think that we want those laws to be observed?" said Dr. Ferris. "We want them broken. You'd better get it straight that it's not a bunch of boy scouts you're up against. We're after power and we mean it. There's no way to rule innocent men. The only power any government has is to crack down on criminals. Well, when there aren't enough criminals, one makes them. One declares so many things to be a crime that it becomes impossible for men to live without breaking laws. Who wants a nation of law-abiding citizens? What's there in that for anyone? But just pass the kind of laws that can neither be observed nor enforced nor objectively interpreted, and you create a nation of law-breakers and then you can cash in. Now that's a system Mr. Rearden, that's the game, and once you understand it, you'll be much easier to deal with."

This excerpt is obviously an extreme way of highlighting the problem, and I'm not looking to voice my political views here, but in some cases this scenario is really quite accurate.

No matter how small your business is, it's vitally important that you educate yourself on whatever laws apply to your business and then comply at all costs. This is especially true in a business-unfriendly state such as California. Small start-ups are often in the dark on all the requirements to stay in compliance, especially when it comes to labor laws.

Some business owners may shrug off the issue, believing that they are simply too insignificant to be on anyone's radar. But the truth is that no matter how small your business is today, any transgression can come back to haunt you tomorrow. If you don't follow labor laws exactly, a disgruntled employee can file a class action lawsuit against you years later, and your company will get dissected back to your first day in business. It's not just the penalties you may receive, but also the cost of defending such a lawsuit, even if you're completely innocent of any wrongdoing. Legal costs can be astronomical, in some cases too much for a business to bear.

Ignoring a license fee can eventually cost many times that amount in penalties. Advertising that's creatively over the edge, with claims that can be rationalized away only in *your* mind, can bring the wrath of authorities down on you. Customer service that doesn't do everything possible to resolve a customer's gripe can create expensive lawsuits and/or bad press. Not having the right legal structure or not respecting that you and your business are separate entities can open you up to personal liability, making yourself a target for bottom-feeding attorneys regardless of whether you did anything wrong.

Once you've reached a point of success, you'll be swimming with sharks who want to take a bite out of your earnings. It's become part of the American way, and you need to put up defenses ahead of time.

There simply is no substitute for legal compliance and strategy. Do your homework early on and save yourself a mountain of fees and headaches later. The time and money you spend on tax and legal compliance will allow you to sleep soundly and spend your time growing your business, not defending it.

Lesson #14

Biz plan yourself

Biz plan yourself

Do you know what it is you want to do? Do you know what you are passionate about? How well do you know yourself?

If you have any questions in your mind as to the direction you want to take, then this chapter is for you. There are a couple exercises in this chapter that I use regularly to help me find a new direction whenever I need it.

As you've heard me say several times, it is vital that you do something you love. If you love what you do, you'll have the energy to get up in the morning, and you'll look forward to going to work. You'll also never hesitate to work late when you need to because you love doing whatever it is you're doing.

It also helps to do something that's intrinsically good. Your activity should provide a product or service that solves a problem for many people or helps them in some way.

When you love what you do, your chances of excellence and success multiply many times over. You'll give yourself the opportunity to excel and be the best in your field. Constant improvement will come naturally as you won't have to force yourself to keep learning, keep practicing, and keep persisting until you make it.

Surprisingly, many people don't know what they love. They may have hobbies that they enjoy, but not all hobbies are conducive to being converted into a thriving business. Can you make money at pretty much anything? Yes, definitely. But not every activity is capable of turning you into a millionaire. It has to be commercially viable. Most are, but a few aren't.

What you love to do doesn't necessarily have to be a specific type of business. It can, however, be the foundation for a business. For example, if you love to be on stage, there are hundreds of business options that involve some sort of public speaking. If you love the outdoors, then you don't want to sit behind a desk from nine to five. You want to do something that has a connection to nature. Likewise, what you don't like doing is equally important. If you're scared of flying, then you don't want to be a salesperson with a ten-state territory.

So how do you find out what's right for you? The best way is to get to know yourself in ways you never have by asking yourself questions you've probably never been asked before. These questions will analyze your personality, your life, and your likes, as well as activities that you don't like, and so on. With this information in hand, you'll feel much more competent in making the right choice for your future endeavor. You'll also be telling the universe what types of opportunities to deliver to your doorstep, helping you to find the right business that much sooner. In essence, you'll be converting your own uniqueness into a personal business plan. It's time to biz plan yourself.

So here are some questions to write down, contemplate, and respond to, ideally in writing. Some of these may take some serious introspection while the answers to others may come to you almost immediately without any thought whatsoever.

These questions continue to be of major importance to me every time it comes time to find a new business. Loving what I do is by far my most important criterion. The money always follows all on its own.

Focusing on money may occasionally work for some people, but they won't have fulfillment. In the end, you want to be fulfilled, having achieved your goal and your purpose. When you do, money becomes little more than a measurement of success because if you succeed in your endeavor but your business fails to make huge sums of money, you won't care nearly as much as you may think right now. That's fulfillment, doing what you love!

You need to answer this first question with a single word: Who are you?

Let me explain. I was once at a seminar where this question was asked. We were told to write down the first word that came to mind without much thinking. The word that popped into my mind was "teacher." I feel fulfilled when I can impart some unique knowledge to someone who appreciates it, applies it, and makes it work to better his or her life. I love nothing more. In retrospect, another word that uniquely describes me is "creator." I love to invent or create something from nothing. So I'm a teacher and a creator. Who are you? What's the first word that comes to mind? Please write it down.

Next, we have three questions that belong together. Unlike the previous question, each of these questions involves a list of answers. Ask yourself these three questions and make a bullet list underneath each.

What do I like to do?

What don't I like to do?

What am I good at?

What you like to do can involve things like travel, writing, inventing, teaching, etc. What you don't like to do can include things like public speaking, flying, being alone, etc. Examples of what you are good at may involve managing, solving problems, sports, selling, negotiating, etc. The options are endless, and everyone's list is going to be substantially different from anyone else's.

Another idea is to make a list of things you love. This has a less direct influence on your future endeavor but can nonetheless provide useful clues. Include anything that comes to mind like driving, flowers, sunsets, sushi — you name it. Even a life list, also known as a bucket list, can provide clues. These are things you'd love to accomplish in your lifetime. They can even include places you'd like to visit, jumping out of an airplane, having children, publishing a book, etc.

Once you've made these lists — and they may take days or weeks to complete — you'll have a unique chance to look at yourself objectively and get to know yourself in a unique new way. These lists can be very useful in determining if a venture or an idea is right for you.

These are also lists you should refer back to regularly. You may add to them at any time or make any modifications that feel right. Not only will you get to know yourself in a new way, but your lists will actually help you pinpoint opportunities that are well suited to you.

Lesson #15

Business strategies

Business strategies

This chapter contains several topics, each describing an approach to doing business that I learned from mentors, observation, trial and error, and reading — lots of reading. I've applied and tested each of them. They involve approaches to doing business that can make a world of difference to your success. Experience has taught me that these include some of the best business advice anyone can give you. Follow them and you'll supercharge your company's potential.

If you want the best for you and your company, don't consider these strategies to be optional. The best entrepreneurs incorporate them into their business strategy from the start to create the best possible business outcome. You can see them applied in some of the greatest companies in the world. But they're also not just for business. They're also for you personally if you want to succeed in all aspects of your life. Always keep in mind that success is not just about money.

Some of these concepts are rather simple to understand, so they don't need to be expanded into a full chapter with numerous examples to illustrate a point. But don't let the simplicity of a concept fool you. Its effect can be profound.

The first is this: Once you decide to move forward with your idea, your first strategy should be one of massive action. That is, go at it with everything you've got. Massive action creates momentum, and that's what you need to propel you forward and keep you motivated. Bill Gates acknowledged that he built Microsoft with massive, immediate action. The momentum you create will make you feel like you're going places — and you are. It will therefore keep you motivated as you won't be chasing success. Success will come visibly closer each day.

Once you've made the decision to pursue a particular goal, go at it with all your heart and put all your time and resources into it. If you don't, someone else will.

Next, to be a great company tomorrow you have to start acting like one today. In our modern world, technologies that once were extremely expensive and therefore exclusive to only those who could afford them are now affordably available to everyone. An example is book printing. The ease and cost-effectiveness of being able to print a book has changed dramatically over the years. It used to be that you had to print so many thousands of copies to get any kind of reasonable cost per unit. Now you can print a single book cheaply, and you can print it when you need it without having to print numerous copies ahead of time.

The point is that everyone has affordable access to a great image. This involves your business cards and stationary, a professional-looking online presence, and everything that the world sees from the outside looking in. With all that we have at our disposal, there's simply no excuse for a second-rate production.

When you look at a website, do you not instantly notice whether a website has been properly thought out and professionally produced? This has a huge impact on whether you'll order from a company. Make your business look like it has already arrived, and your potential customers will hit that order button with a lot less hesitation.

The same goes for you. Dress professionally, speak professionally, and act like you've already succeeded. That is, show confidence and quality in everything the world sees. I once made the mistake of showing up at a high-level negotiation in cowboy boots and a trench coat. I later found out that some attendees questioned whether I was a real businessman. I thought my outfit demonstrated individualism. It did, but so do nose piercings and tattoos up to your eyeballs. Obviously, none of those are wise choices in business.

Acting like you've already succeeded does not mean showing off. It means finding the right balance. Would you buy an expensive product from a stranger driving a thirty-year-old beat-up clunker? Probably not because something tells you there's a problem, and he's obviously not successful. It looks like no one has ever bought anything from him. He can't even afford a decent car. Likewise, would you buy that same product from someone showing up in a Rolls Royce talking a tall game? This would also make most people think twice as his markup is probably a rip-off. Why else is he driving a half-million-dollar car and telling you repeatedly how wonderful he is?

Find a happy medium that makes your customer comfortable doing business with you. People like being around successful people, but they don't like being around show-offs or the opposite extreme, people who look like they don't know what they're doing.

Finally, I'd like to introduce a Japanese principle to you called Kaizen. It's one of those precious little nuggets that has enormous power even if you don't recognize it right away. In fact, many consider it to be the reason for Japan's economic superiority during the eighties.

Kaizen is the practice of continual incremental improvement, mostly small but regular — even daily — improvements. These improvements can be in any area of the company, whether it's in technology, customer service, management, product quality, etc.

Here's how I implemented the principle of Kaizen in one of my companies. During every one of our weekly meetings, each employee was required to make one suggested improvement in any aspect of the company, no matter how small the improvement. We would then vote on each suggestion and immediately implement those we all agreed upon. By practicing Kaizen, my company got better each week. Even if the improvements were small, over time they added up to major improvements in our work environment and competitiveness. It worked.

The theory is that a company that does not continually innovate and improve is standing still. This is the result of complacency, and complacency is business death. In business, standing still is the same as going backwards. If you're not getting better all the time, I guarantee you, one or more of your competitors is getting better, and they will overtake you.

Kaizen is not only incredibly effective, it's also fun. It gets your employees involved in the progress of the company and thereby creates a bond of loyalty. I highly recommend it in your business and in your life.

Act successful, like your company has already arrived. Success breeds more success. Massive, immediate action will launch your company forward and leave the competition behind. Combine those actions with never-ending incremental improvements and you'll be incorporating three very powerful tools into your arsenal.

Destiny:

The final lesson

Destiny

This final chapter is very personal. It's the story of one of my greatest successes and one of my greatest downfalls, all in one business. It is in the events of the following pages that I learned some of the lessons described throughout this book, but that's not why I included this chapter. I included this chapter because I believe the events in this story to be connected — and not by chance. This creates a teachable moment. In fact, some of these events came about in such an uncanny fashion that I believe I was guided from above. There's just no other way for me to make sense of it all. I believe I was guided in order to learn the lessons that I needed to learn, and I was guided because the concept I created was meant to happen. I became the vehicle that brought this new concept into the world and into the lives of many people who benefitted as a result.

You should know that you are guided also and that the successes and failures you experience in your life happen for a reason. I believe we give ourselves these lessons, predetermined before we are born. We know what lessons we need to learn in order to advance to a higher level of existence. Once we learn a lesson, we move on to the next lesson. If we don't learn it, then we start again, but the outcome will be more severe each time we ignore the lesson until we do learn and are ready to move on. Remember that lessons learned involve change, change in our lives and change in our character.

As I mentioned, this is a very personal story. It's also somewhat embarrassing in parts because it involves a government lawsuit that, on the surface, doesn't look very good. Nonetheless, it's the greatest thing I've ever done, and it will influence my career and character for the rest of my life.

I'll use all the actual names of companies and people involved. I won't leave anything out. I'll leave it up to you to form your own opinion from an unedited account of actual events without rewriting history. Hopefully you'll see what I see and maybe see what inspired some of the previous insights. If you learn from this chapter that your life is most certainly guided and that your failures are also blessings, then the risk I take in sharing this with you is worth it.

I'm including this chapter mainly because of a common thread you may have noticed throughout some of the chapters in this book. Part of being an entrepreneur is being an innovator. Innovation comes from inspiration, and inspiration comes from somewhere inside us that's connected to somewhere beyond us. As I always say, when I ask something of the universe, the universe always provides. And that's because I've learned how to ask and to trust that it really will provide. The technique or philosophy I'm referring to is explained in the chapter on goal setting, specifically the underlying foundation within the best-path method.

Whether you think it's the universe that provides, or some space many refer to as the collective unconsciousness, or God, or your angels, or a connection to a universal body of knowledge via your subconscious mind, I don't know exactly which it is. But I do know it exists, and it's there for you to tap into if you believe in it and trust its benevolent ability to help you whenever you call on it. It's often been there for me even when I didn't specifically ask for its guidance. Inspiration sometimes comes out of the blue, but I believe only if you've made prior connections to this body of knowledge. Notice the life-changing moments of inspiration that appeared literally out of nowhere and typically totally unexpected. You have access to all the same.

The following is the story of *The Mentor Network*.

It was just one week after Hurricane Andrew in late August 1992, and I was elated that the Bahamian Islands were still on the map. My three-day weekend with Mary wouldn't be cancelled. Mary flew in from California to meet me in Ft. Lauderdale, Florida, where we would immediately continue on to Paradise Island in the Bahamas. Paradise Island was owned by Merv Griffin and comes closest to manifesting its name than any other island I've ever been to.

Mary and I stayed at the Ocean Club Hotel, built on the grounds of an ancient twelfth-century Augustinian cloister. The grounds were as beautiful and romantic as any Impressionist artist would have us imagine, except that the canvas was the real world, not a painting, meticulously created to transport us into Camelot. I most vividly remember the ancient headless statues and ruins at the end of a lawn the size of a football field. If a rose has no other duty except to be beautiful, then this retreat was a rose garden.

I had met Mary in a Thai restaurant in West Los Angeles called Chan Dara. She was the hostess. Our introduction consisted of a rather crude correction of what little Thai I knew at the time.

In a letter I received from Mary weeks after our vacation, she described our vacation thus: "... the many shades of blue, nature's work, the green that enveloped us in Eden ...." Mary was attending UCLA at the time. She's Vietnamese, gorgeous, and grew up attending classes for especially gifted students. That weekend, though I didn't know it at the time, Mary changed my life.

On the last evening on Paradise Island, we took a sunset stroll along the curved beach in front of our hotel. The scene couldn't have been enhanced in any way. It was Paradise Island. As we chatted about nothing in particular, a transient — the only other person to be seen anywhere — approached us asking for money. It was obvious that the money would be used for alcohol. (Incidentally, the local beer, called Kalik, is excellent.)

Shaking my head, I told the transient sorry, but no. As we passed him, Mary asked me why I didn't give him a few dollars. I asked her why I should. It wouldn't help him. We both knew he'd use it to get drunk. She said I should have given him money to show that I cared. My forehead immediately wrinkled into a disbelieving frown. Mary proceeded to tell me about her unending sympathy and caring for the unemployed, poor, and underprivileged. She claimed to be a true champion for the underdog.

I told her that I felt sympathy for the underprivileged also, but that I chose not to express it with token gestures that offered no real benefit to anyone. Mary disagreed vehemently with my "lack of compassion." She insisted that she cared more than I did and that it was not a matter of trying to solve a problem, but an expression of sympathy that would cause her to give away her last dollar (more winkles on my forehead). Lovely. Solving the problem seemed irrelevant as long as we all cared. And Mary was convinced that I didn't care.

The discussion that followed between Mary and me remained in the back of my mind for years. It marked the first time I was able to express beliefs that had always been a part of me but had never found a verbal outlet. I was in my late twenties at the time as I argued on the side of saving our dollars until there were enough of them to accomplish something real, lasting, and worthwhile — that is, teaching someone to fish versus just giving someone a fish. I argued that if we spend each dollar as it comes in, we'll never go beyond little gestures designed to help no one but ourselves feel good about how much we care. Nothing would ever get solved that way. Mary didn't agree.

My beliefs were not concisely defined yet, and I was struggling to articulate what was aching to burst out from within me. Nonetheless, I was bothered by the self-righteousness I found in Mary's defense of feelings over actions, symbolism over substance. In later years I found this same system of beliefs and self-righteous attitude everywhere I looked. It was pure liberalism although I didn't know it at the time.

After multiple periods of introspection, it occurred to me that I had a pretty firm set of convictions. The first time these convictions took form beyond merely an intuitive feeling was in 1991. Someone recommended I read *Atlas Shrugged* by Ayn Rand. I still believe it to be one of the greatest books ever written, and now, whenever a book is recommended to me, I pay close attention. The two most influential books in my life, *Atlas Shrugged* and *The Path of Least Resistance*, were both recommendations from other people.

Atlas Shrugged spoke from within me and showed me that self-interest is only destructive when it's at the expense of someone else. It is an entirely constructive motivator, completely in harmony with nature, when it results in the benefit of others. We can only take care of others after we take care of ourselves. I learned that there's a vast difference between rational self-interest and mindless self-indulgence.

I was no longer alone. Upon learning that *Atlas Shrugged* was the second-most influential book in America, second only to the Bible, it became evident that there had to be others who shared my beliefs. Nonetheless, I still didn't have an easy answer regarding how to put my beliefs into practice.

Going back in time a little more, it was as early as 1987 that the question in search of an answer first appeared from out of nowhere. I was in my early twenties, successful in sales, and master of my universe. One day I decided to do something worthwhile for the less fortunate and became the proud sponsor of five needy children through an organization that was then called Foster Parents Plan and also through Christian Children's Fund (CCF). When I sponsored these children, I immediately pondered, why sponsor five children and not just one? In retrospect, I think it was an attempt to, within my means, make a greater difference.

An interesting thing happened to me when I received the pictures of the children I was sponsoring at about twenty dollars per month each. I didn't feel it was enough. I examined my motives and found that I wanted to help these innocent little children, but I was doing it for myself also. I was trying to make myself feel like I was doing something worthwhile and that I was making a difference. But it wasn't enough. I felt that helping even as many as five kids was merely a token gesture to soothe my conscience. This made me feel guilty, even selfish in a way I didn't like.

The issue immediately begged its case: how many children would I have to support to really make a difference, where the difference would be large enough so that my selfish motives would become irrelevant by virtue of a substantial positive end result? At what point did the end justify satisfying a selfish motive?

It may have sounded a bit Machiavellian, but at that time in my life, it was probably as good a rationalization as any to make the good outweigh the bad. Based on what I'd been taught as a child, I thought that selfish motives of all kinds were bad, and some of that still stuck with me. Although I had not yet read *Atlas Shrugged*, the answer seemed obvious enough. I needed to sponsor 100–200 children. Then I would be doing enough good in the world where my motives to make myself feel better became essentially irrelevant.

Then I did the math. Two hundred sponsorships multiplied by twenty dollars for each child equals four thousand dollars per month! So much for that idea. But I didn't give up. The solution seemed to be to somehow become responsible for the sponsorship of two hundred children, even if I didn't personally sponsor them all — that is, to get others to sponsor children in sufficient numbers.

I had an idea. I had always had the dream of having a very large company one day with numerous employees. Therefore, if I managed to build a company with hundreds of employees, I could then go to them before the holidays and ask them to join me in an act of compassion and encourage each of them to sponsor a child. If I could convince enough of my employees to follow me in this, I could achieve my goal of getting several hundred needy children sponsored. But how long would this take? Much too long. Besides, I would be able to afford the four thousand dollars per month long before any company of mine was large enough to have that many employees. This was obviously not the right answer. But the question stayed in the back of my mind for years, patiently waiting, for I was convinced that one day the right answer would reveal itself.

The cornerstone event happened in 1993 when I found the answer to my problem. How can I make a real difference in the world? How can I become responsible for the sponsorship of 100–200 children? It turned out that the answer involved a very creative application of constructive self-interest.

In October 1993, I founded The Mentor Network, Inc., a network marketing company. Mentor began as a book-of-the-month program for success-oriented books reprinted in a collector's format. The collection was designed to look similar to the Great Books Series by Britannica. Each month a subscriber would receive one of the great books of success to add to their growing collection. From Dale Carnegie and Earl Nightingale to Napoleon Hill and Tony Robbins, they would all be included in the greatest library of success ever created.

It was the discovery of an unexpected loophole in the publishing world — a minor miracle in and of itself — that allowed me to reprint the blockbusters of personal development and success. Although these were some of the best-selling books of all time, with their licenses locked up for decades to come, the licenses to reprint them in a collector's format were largely available. Who knew? My first license was obtained from Simon & Schuster for *How to Win Friends and Influence People.* I was not only incredibly grateful that I managed to discover this loophole and obtain this license, but I was also in business.

Mentor was conceived for two reasons. First, the potential behind network or multilevel marketing fascinated me. It seemed to be the ultimate combination of compounded growth and leverage. The mathematical principles that made it work left me spellbound. As always, having no knowledge or prior experience in a field never deterred me from diving in headfirst. I loved the challenge. The second reason was that Mentor allowed me to get into the personal-development business. I consider myself a product of self-help information, so it gave me an opportunity to grow further by teaching and passing on the wisdom that helped me achieve success in the past.

One of the greatest joys in life for me has always been teaching. I am by nature a teacher and most of all I love to teach people how to succeed in their professional lives. An eager audience and the opportunity to see individuals grow as a result of my help have always given me an incredible feeling of contribution and self-worth. Mentor gave me the vehicle to do just that.

Looking back, I started Mentor quite by accident (another uncanny coincidence). I had created a blueprint for my idea almost one year prior, but it was just that and nothing more, another idea. I'm not sure I really had the intention of turning it into reality. The decision to start the company was the result of a young military cadet named Jeff Nordstrom coming to my home one day to pick up a secondhand item I was selling. When he entered my home, he immediately sat down in front of my desk and asked me if I could be his mentor (maybe that's why I named the company Mentor). He said that he saw my car outside, which convinced him I was successful. He wanted to leave the military but had no business skills and little savings. He was looking for someone to guide his way.

I was completely caught off guard but didn't want to disappoint Jeff with a lack of answers. Maybe I also had something to prove to myself at that time. Plus, here was a willing student waiting for his teacher to appear. That was a golden opportunity I wasn't about to give up.

I told Jeff that I had been contemplating opening a network marketing company and explained how you could make a lot of money building a referral network. I explained my whole concept of a book-of-the-month club and asked if he wanted to participate. He said he had six months of military service left in Georgia, but upon his return he'd be immediately ready to join. Although I had no idea at the time how I would get licenses to reprint the books I needed for the series, I told him it would take six months for me to get everything ready, so our timing was perfect. Without hesitation we shook hands. Mentor was born, and we opened on schedule exactly six months later. Jeff became my first distributor.

The world of network marketing was infinitely more complex and competitive than I imagined. This didn't bother me although growth was excruciatingly slow at first. What bothered me was that something was missing. I felt it but didn't know what it was. Then it dawned on me. The company lacked a true driving force, a mission.

I was sitting on my couch one day in my rented apartment in Newport Beach, California, overlooking the bluffs of the Back Bay area. My living room was partially converted into an office, and an adjacent spare bedroom was by then filled with books from floor to ceiling. You had to walk through little canyons made of books to move around. If they had been on the second floor, the weight of all those books would have collapsed the floor.

That day the TV was on and I was going through my mail. I had already removed my bills and was left with only junk mail. One of the envelopes was from Children International, another child-sponsorship company. I immediately thought, "One of these days I should sponsor children again."

As I opened the envelope, I discarded the sales letter and looked at the order form. My eyes went right to the price line. It cost $24 per month to sponsor a child. In that instant my life changed. In a flash of divine intervention that lasted only about one thousandth of a second, I made the connection that a child sponsorship was nothing more than any other subscription program, essentially identical to my company's book-of-the-month program. Theirs was $24 per month, mine was $30 per month, but both were essentially continuity programs. Why not market child sponsorships through network marketing and become responsible for sponsoring 200 children that way? Brilliant!

That day I found not only my mission for The Mentor Network but also the solution to the problem that had been shadowing me for years. The means to support 200 children was right in front of me. The surge of energy this insight gave me was indescribable.

Once the initial elation subsided, I was left with a feeling of being all revved up with no place to go because I had no clue how to bring child sponsorships into the world of network marketing. I knew nothing about the charitable industry, nor did I know if it would work in the first place. Heck, I hadn't even turned Mentor into a successful network marketing company yet. Then I wondered; would others even like this idea? I couldn't even tell anyone about it for fear that someone would run with my idea before I had the chance to turn it into reality. My mind was racing, and there were walls blocking me in every direction.

My idea to market child sponsorships through multilevel marketing became not only my moral mission for Mentor but also my most cherished secret for the next two years. The first time I ever mentioned my concept to anyone with any coherency was to my family when I visited them in Germany. As with any idea brought to friends and family that didn't involve becoming a doctor or a lawyer, their support was underwhelming to say the least. They quickly came up with several reasons it wouldn't — no, why it couldn't — work.

The greatest opposition came from my younger sister. She was very adamant about this being exploitation of needy children. Huh? That's new! I didn't see it that way at all. How can you exploit someone who doesn't have anything? How can you exploit someone by helping them? Though I love my sister very much, I was very disturbed by her uncompromising display of self-righteousness (she must have "cared" more than I did). My parents were slightly more accepting. They gave a cautious "hmm" to my idea. Oh well.

Shortly thereafter I had a very vivid dream. In my dream I was a tank, like a military Sherman tank. I was on a mountain path with a several-thousand-foot drop on my left and a steep wall on my right. Clouds and mountain mist were all around. The path was clogged with vegetation, making it almost impenetrable. Vines were hanging over the path from the wall on my right, making forward momentum virtually impossible. Any sane person would have turned back, thinking there was no way to get through the knotted vegetation. I didn't. I plowed forward with all my strength. Although I was a tank in my dream, it still took tremendous effort. Nothing was going to stop me.

I did make it through despite trees, shrubs, and vines blocking my way. It was a test of my willpower. When I woke, I realized immediately what the dream meant. I had a difficult road ahead. My subconscious was telling me not to give up, to plow ahead. It would take willpower and tremendous persistence. If I continued trying, I would prevail. Since I don't recall many dreams and especially not ones that have such clear significance, I paid particular attention to this message.

I still didn't realize the potential of sponsoring children through network marketing until I made an appointment with World Vision, the largest child sponsorship company in the world. Ed Gruman, the gentleman in charge of analyzing third-party marketing proposals, was incredibly encouraging. We first chatted about my book series, which he really loved. Then I told him about my idea to market child sponsorships through our organization. My passion must have been obvious. His eyes lit up.

His final statement to me said it all. "Look behind you," he said. I did. There was a huge filing cabinet. "For three years I've been collecting and analyzing third-party marketing proposals for World Vision. That cabinet is full of hundreds of them. I've learned to separate the wheat from the chaff.

Listening to your idea, I know I'm looking at the wheat. I have a feeling we'll be doing business together."

Ed committed to bringing my idea to the circle of vice presidents. He also cautioned me not to expect any immediate results. World Vision is an enormous company with an equally enormous bureaucracy. It would take time. Ed told me he would be retiring within a year, and it would be his parting gesture to get me the audience I deserved.

Ed was right. That was my first encounter with the world of nonprofits. What most people don't realize is that charities are businesses like any other, with the same problems, competition, and challenges that for-profit companies have to deal with. In fact, because nonprofits often rely on grants, generosity, and donations, competition can be even fiercer, red tape even more of a hurdle.

When a nonprofit gets to be the size of World Vision, with almost a half-billion dollars in annual revenues, I had to accept that I was dealing with a behemoth. None of this mattered to me, however. I found someone who loved my idea. That's all I could think about. Even if there would never be a relationship between Mentor and World Vision, I was now convinced that my concept was viable.

The next step in my odyssey came just a few months later while attending a business forum called Income Builders International (IBI). IBI is a weeklong seminar that teaches entrepreneurs how to make their dreams come true. In the process of learning the required business skills and strategies, one is also taught a proprietary technique of networking that allows you to make the contacts you need while still at the forum. No matter what kind of contact you seek — an expert, investor, or someone who knows Oprah — you can be assured that you'll find it at IBI. IBI was probably the best entrepreneurial boot camp in the world, and their multimedia Superteaching technology is highly entertaining and often a life-changing turning point for its students and faculty alike.

I had attended the forum several times, and I was welcome to market Mentor's book program at IBI, partially because the owner, Bernard Dohrmann, personally knew many of the authors in my book series from his childhood. Since Mr. Dohrmann's father was one of the individuals responsible for helping to create the self-help industry, the early greats of the industry stayed at their house frequently. Mentor ended up being very much loved by students and faculty alike.

Early in 1995, one of IBI's instructors, Mitch Santell, decided to probe a little deeper into my motives. While we were sitting at a hotel bar enjoying a drink, he asked me what my plans were for the company. I told him he already knew, to grow my book-of-the-month series. He stared at me and said he knew me better than that. There had to be something more profound going on in my world. I asked him if he could keep a secret. He said yes, so I told him about my idea of bringing child sponsorships into network marketing, and I told him about my encounter with World Vision. He was visibly impressed.

Barely one hour later, Mitchell was on stage teaching a class on the importance of having a vision and the power of passion. Suddenly I heard my name. He asked if I was in the audience. I was being called to the stage and I had no idea why. (I even looked around to see if there was another Parviz in the audience.) As I got up and walked to the stage, I wondered where I fit into this lesson. Mitchell simply said, "Parviz, tell everyone about your vision for Mentor." I couldn't believe what I was hearing as I looked at him in disbelief. This was supposed to have been a secret. Now I was standing in front of more than 300 people with no choice but to talk.

It was the first time I talked about my child sponsorship idea in public. I virtually froze, but somehow I managed to explain my dream. To this day, I don't recall another instance in my life where I had so much difficulty speaking. The experience was similar to an extreme version of stage fright. Nonetheless, I talked about 35,000 innocent children dying every day, and then I relived my conversation with Ed Gruman from World Vision.

The impact on my audience left me speechless. As I walked back to my seat amidst a standing ovation, I sat down only to find that everyone else was still standing with thundering applause all around me. I looked up and around me and saw what would become a somewhat regular occurrence in the coming years. I saw many wonderful caring people with tears in their eyes. I was incredibly surprised. It was obvious that people really liked my idea — more than that, they loved it.

After Mitchell's class was over, numerous people immediately approached me wanting to either invest in my company or somehow become a part of it. One lady named Kay Doyle told me she knew someone who owned a smaller child sponsorship agency who would likely be delighted to talk to me about my idea. She wanted to know if I was interested in talking to the owner. YES!

Within ten days, I had a signed contract from Childcare International out of Bellingham, Washington. Mentor would become their marketing agent using network marketing to market child sponsorships for the first time ever. Instead of spending a fortune on advertising to attract sponsors of needy children, we would pay our sponsors referral fees when they brought us new sponsors.

I didn't realize until later that the partnership between Childcare International and me was in itself a miracle. Max Lange, the president of Childcare, called me months later to tell me why he took this leap of faith with me. He told me that prior to my first contact with him, he prayed for a means to support 50,000 children one day, and I was his answer from God. Wow!

To this day, I'm still amazed at the sequence of events that led to MentorVision (the name of our child sponsorship program). But it was only the beginning. The best was yet to come when I began to realize the significance of my discovery. What started as a solution to a problem I was trying to solve for myself turned out to be a solution to something so much greater than myself. Had I known the significance right from the start, it may have never happened. I would have been overwhelmed with responsibility and probably stumbled over endless self-imposed limitations. As it turned out, I became a voice for a concept that had to happen, no matter what. To this day, I still believe that it was in harmony with nature, religion, free enterprise, and reality, working better than much we have tried thus far to cure some of the economic injustices of the world.

Within little over one year, Mentor was providing food, clothing, and education for over 2,300 needy children worldwide using an unproven concept in an industry where I had no experience whatsoever. Our goal became the sponsorship of one million children. It would take us about ten to twelve years, an accomplishment that took World Vision more than sixty years using conventional fund-raising means. In the process we would provide an income to countless families here in the U.S.

As for myself, I felt better about what I was doing than ever before. I took my message of compassionate capitalism on the road and made plans to expand our concept. We were ready to sponsor American kids on Indian reservations. Plans to start an animal support program and a tree-planting program were also getting close to reality. We wanted to give our sponsors the choice of participating in that which most touched their hearts, needy children, abandoned animals, or the environment: Childcare, Animalcare, and Ecocare.

I found that there were two types of people in our world. The first group found out about us and said, "Where have you been all my life? This is exactly what I've been looking for. I *have to* get involved!" The other group wondered if we were making money off needy children. Even when we explained in a thousand different ways that we were making a living by helping children, they still didn't get it. And I didn't get them.

Was it about the money? Yes, partially. But here's the difference. Isn't it better to make a living doing something worthwhile? Shouldn't our free enterprise system reward those who do good? And shouldn't we support a system where the more good one does, the more one gets rewarded? Even if I tried, I couldn't make myself think any different. I had all the answers I needed every time I looked at one of the pictures of a sponsored child or when I read a letter from one of our distributors thanking us profoundly for giving purpose to their family after becoming distributors in Mentor. We continued to get more and more needy kids sponsored until we became responsible for fully one-third of Childcare International's revenues.

My dream came to an abrupt end on November 6, 1996, when the Federal Trade Commission shut down Mentor. They walked into my company while I was at a meeting negotiating the details for sponsoring American kids on Indian reservations. My assistant called me and told me that a group of officials with badges walked into my office and took over, telling everyone to leave. The FTC froze all my business and personal assets and handed me a lawsuit three inches thick, alleging that I had violated network marketing statutes. I was specifically told that I was not even allowed to use my credit card to buy food for myself or anything else. They left me with $20 in cash.

The government completely froze my life. In that moment I became like a blind man who's afraid of the dark. I couldn't see any way out of my personal hell, and suddenly I was totally alone in the world.

The Federal Trade Commission's allegation was that a child sponsorship was not a product, and therefore Mentor was an illegal pyramid. I was told that they had no problem with my book-of-the-month program because it was considered a real product.

I later discovered that we fell into a sting operation to take out several blatantly bad MLM programs. The FTC also thought we were much bigger than we were, and they assumed the money wasn't going to the kids. When the court-appointed receiver audited every penny of the company, he and his crew did not find a single misappropriated dollar. However, the same receiver had the legal right to pay himself out of our company checking account. He decided to pay himself $65,000 for sitting in my office for a month as he looked for dirt. We actually had several pleasant conversations, and I could tell he liked me. But when I saw how he raped my company's bank account, I felt doubly betrayed.

In retrospect, I now also know how my rights were blatantly violated by the government. My personal assets were frozen so that I wouldn't be able to afford an adequate defense. Today, having been a political radio talk show host for more than two years and actually understanding my rights, I know that if I knew then what I know now, I would have fought back.

My attorney hired an economist to prove that a child sponsorship was a real product. The results seemed kind of obvious to me. An intangible product is still a product. Taking out Mentor was clearly a mistake, and everyone knew it. I still believe, however, that there was more to it than I may ever know. Someone felt threatened by us and applied pressure to shut down our system. Maybe it worked too well. The proof was in their statement. There was no problem with our book-of-the-month program. They made this very clear. Yet it was structured identically to the child sponsorship program — same price and same compensation structure. The ONLY difference was that one was tangible and the other was not. That's clearly not enough of a dispute to justify putting 2,300 children back on the streets. Obviously there was another reason to shut us down that had nothing to do with legal standing.

One of the things that caused me special grief was how this was treated in the press. I was interviewed several times and not a single word of what I said was ever printed. The reporters just wanted dirt, and they printed whatever they wanted to create the story they wanted. It's common knowledge that bad news sells, so it's naïve to think that the press will ever be objective. In retrospect, I feel nothing but disgust for the journalist scumbags who make money by printing dirt while we made money by saving children. Yet it was my life that was shredded.

Despite receiving hundreds of letters of support (which we provided to the court), and proving our case, in the end I had little choice but to settle with them. The government doesn't like to lose, and I couldn't afford the half-million dollars in legal fees it would take to win. Settling was my only option. The end result was that they took everything, and I signed a consent decree promising not to do certain things that I never did in the first place. In return, the consent decree included a statement (at my insistence) that child sponsorships can be marketed via network marketing and that I can go back into business doing essentially the same thing. With that inclusion I felt that I had made history by putting our system on the map. Other companies immediately picked up on it and built sizeable organizations supporting needy kids around the world.

Unfortunately this tragedy ruined my company. It wiped me out financially and put 2,300 children back on the streets, in addition to the emotional hell it put me through. Nonetheless, I felt a certain victory when I was allowed to rebuild. I called the chief prosecutor at the FTC and told him that I wanted to go back into business. Would they bother me again? His exact answer to me was, "Oh no, go ahead. We only mess with you once."

So I rebuilt, or I should say I tried. I reopened Mentor under a different name and promptly shut down three weeks later. I couldn't do it. I didn't have it in me and didn't realize at that time what they had done to me. They took away that which I loved the most, and in the process they destroyed my spirit. For one full year I was incapable of working. Several friends had already abandoned me thinking that I must have done something wrong or this would have never happened. I became more and more desensitized. I remember taking an ice cube out of the freezer, and as I turned around, it occurred to me that I couldn't tell whether it was hot or cold. My doctor tried to put me on antidepressants and my life felt empty.

Maybe everything happens for a reason. Although I still don't know who or what happened behind the scenes to cause my company to be shut down, and I may never know, the concept of Mentor led to something equally profound years later.

It all started with a movie called *Dear God*. In the story, actor Greg Kinnear plays a misfit that gets in trouble with the law. His punishment is that he has to get a job. He ends up working in the back of a post office where the majority of employees are either recluses or in some way outcasts from society.

Each year the post office gets tens of thousands of letters addressed to God and Santa Claus. Per federal law, even the post office is not allowed to throw away or tamper with mail, so it accumulates into giant piles of unopened letters. Greg Kinnear and his crew of misfits eventually succumb to their curiosity and start to read some of these letters. At first, they ridiculed the people who wrote them for writing letters to God and Santa. Most of the letters expressed a wish or some sort of despair.

Eventually some of the letters touched this group of postal employees on a deeper emotional level. They decided to make some of the wishes come true, and throughout the movie they even managed to save the life of one letter's author who wrote a desperate suicide note to God.

The wish they granted that particularly caught my attention was to a homeless man they knew. This man sold the only worldly possession he treasured, his beloved saxophone, so that he could buy food. His plea to God was for a new sax. Greg and his cohorts decide to bring the homeless man a new saxophone, and they slipped it into his arms while he was sleeping in the park. That is, they did it anonymously.

"Wow," I thought, "what a great concept, granting wishes anonymously." I was fascinated by the idea of doing good without there being any possibility for receiving anything in return, not even a thank you. Would that eliminate the stain of selfishness?

I wondered; where could I find a regular supply of wishes and dreams? Could I become friendly with my mail carrier to get access to Dear God letters? Probably not. Could I join a prayer group in my local church and make people's prayers come true anonymously? Nothing is impossible, but these ideas were easier said than done. Once again I found myself carrying around an idea for several years ... and then I saw another movie.

Pay It Forward is a magnificently touching and impactful film. The emotions it brings forth, especially at the end, are profound. The concept portrayed in the movie was simple. When someone does you a favor, don't pay it back, pay it forward instead to someone new and tell them to do the same. In this way a self-perpetuating cycle of favors and good deeds is done by more and more people with no expectation of receiving anything in return.

I don't know why it happened or how it happened, but the concepts of anonymous giving, as portrayed in *Dear God*, plus the pay-it-forward concept from the movie by the same name, needed to merge. I wanted to create a pay-it-forward concept of anonymous good deeds. This time, creating what I envisioned seemed so challenging that I just had to make it a reality. The near impossible was just too intriguing to let it languish in the back of my mind any longer.

The process would be to find someone in need with a specific wish. We would make it come true anonymously, essentially delivering it to their doorstep and surprising them. The only thing they would find except for the gift would be a business card that said "Compliments of Dreamweavers," and a web address. When they visited the website out of curiosity, it would tell them that we don't wish to be contacted and aren't looking for a thank you. The only thing we want is for them to do a good deed for someone else, paying it forward. The website also provided them with the verbiage for a note they could leave that would motivate their gift recipient to also pay it forward.

My plan was to start a nonprofit with a suitable name and web address. Back at Income Builders International (IBI) I used my network to build a board of directors for my new nonprofit consisting of several attorneys, an accountant, and myself. I thought that if the Federal Trade Commission has a problem with me giving anonymous gifts, they can deal with a board of directors of attorneys that will protect our company.

Dreamweavers was born, and to my absolute delight I managed to reserve www.randomactsofkindness.org for its web address. I still had no idea how to actually set the whole thing in motion by finding and fulfilling cases, but I knew it would resolve itself as things always do in my world.

My first challenge appeared almost instantaneously. I received threatening letters from the attorneys for the Random Acts of Kindness Foundation demanding that I release the domain name. I immediately contacted one of the attorneys on our board (the same attorney who represented me against the FTC years before). He advised me to go speak with our resident intellectual property attorney who was teaching at IBI at the time. I knew Maria Speth well and met her in her hotel room.

I first swore Maria to secrecy since my original concept involved total anonymity, including my involvement as its founder. That later proved to be a little unrealistic since someone had to promote the idea, but for years thereafter I still didn't discuss Dreamweavers unless there was good reason to. Once Maria agreed to secrecy, I mentioned that I started a nonprofit. Within an instant she replied, "Dreamweavers?"

"Yes, how did you know?" I replied with a blank stare.

"I was just trying to make a donation to it online."

I was floored. Word was spreading already, and all we had was a website. Considering the serendipity of the situation, I asked Maria to join our board of directors, and she agreed without hesitation. Now I had three attorneys on our board. Cool.

Next, we tackled the issue of the letter I received from the Random Acts of Kindness Foundation. Maria looked up their trademark online and concluded that they weren't very skilled in protecting their intellectual property and that I had nothing to worry about. She would handle the situation and ensure that I could continue using the domain name. She fulfilled her promise without delay.

Although Dreamweavers has never been very active in finding and fulfilling cases because it was essentially a one-man show, it has nonetheless completed enough cases to demonstrate the undeniable viability of the concept. Once we even received a $20,000 donation to help fund cases.

Most cases fell into the $500 to $800 range. We found a schoolteacher with three kids who had a washer but couldn't afford a dryer. We magically made a new dryer appear on her front lawn. We found a handicapped family on the East Coast whose wish was to visit Florida. We sent them plane tickets anonymously. We paid for a chemo treatment, and we paid for the repair of a car. We found an artistically talented teenager whose parents couldn't afford art supplies. We had them mailed to the family anonymously. We even bought a puppy for a deserving young girl.

Within a few years, we fulfilled many more wishes. Some were referrals, some were nominations that came from a form on our website, and some came from newspaper articles. The only rule for nominations was that you couldn't be related to the person you were nominating.

Finding cases was actually more difficult than one might imagine, but the bottom line was always the same for me: even if this remains a self-funded one man show, that's still good enough.

Here's the connection to Mentor that suddenly crystallized out of nowhere in my mind. Dreamweavers was the exact 180-degree opposite to Mentor. Mentor participants made money by helping people. At Dreamweavers nobody got paid a dime for helping others. Mentor was built on the premise of changing the world. Dreamweavers didn't claim anything. We did good deeds only because it was the right thing to do, even if it was something as simple as paying the toll for the car behind you. At Mentor I was very vocal about our belief in compassionate capitalism. Dreamweavers was largely anonymous, and I didn't talk about it unless I needed to. At Mentor we talked about selfish motives being okay. At Dreamweavers we cut off the possibility of even getting a thank you. Dreamweavers was built on the biblical premise that if you tell, it doesn't count.

Dreamweavers doesn't exist any longer as life had other projects for me to pursue. Nonetheless, the impact The Mentor Network and Dreamweavers had on my life and the lessons I learned are profound and will last a lifetime. I'm especially grateful for the proof these two companies provided me in how the universe always provides key pivotal events to move us in the direction that's right for us, in the process teaching us the lessons we need to learn. Although these events may have seemed like coincidences at the time, when you view such an incredible series of coincidences and guiding events over the course of many years, it becomes obvious that a much more powerful force is influencing our lives. To me, this is a source of comfort for which I'm endlessly grateful. Now, whenever I create the intention for a new business idea to materialize, I know that it inevitably will. What a wonderful world.

In Gratitude

I would be so grateful if you could take a minute or two to share what you loved about this book and provide an honest review on our Amazon sales page.

About the Author

―――――――――――――――●●●――――――――――――――

For 25 years, Parviz Firouzgar has been the owner of numerous multi-million dollar companies in a variety of industries, sometimes running several ventures simultaneously, both for profit and nonprofit entities. Some of Parviz's companies involved the use of investor funds of up to several million dollars. As mentioned, one investor walked away with $1.7 million dollars in one year as a result of his confidence in the author's abilities when Parviz was just in his 20's.

Parviz founded a mortgage company and employed over 500 loan officers. He wrote business plans for startup companies that helped them raise many millions in startup capital. After he discovered a new way of raising funds, he expanded into the charitable arena. Within one year, his company was supporting 2300 needy children around the world, providing all their food, clothing and education.

Parviz has been in the direct mail and sweepstakes business, mailing so many millions of pieces of mail each month that his local post office had to expand their operations. Most recently, he has been in the precious metals and diamond business, including owning a gold mine.

Parviz was a radio talk show host and a long time instructor for Income Builders International (IBI), now called CEO Space, an entrepreneurial forum with internationally recognized instructors, such as: Jack Canfield, Mark Victor Hansen, Bob Proctor, T. Harv Eker, John Gray and Lisa Nichols.

Raised in Europe, Parviz speaks four languages. He has been accepted for membership in Mensa and Intertel, both high I.Q. societies.

Acknowledgements

There are many people I'll be eternally grateful to, but a few stand out. I would like to thank my first mentor, Kayes Ahmed, who not only believed in the potential of my drive and passion but who also became the first person to ever invest in me. He was truly an incredible person and fabulously effective business leader.

Secondly, I would like to extend my heartfelt gratitude to Berny Dohrmann, founder of CEO Space (formerly called IBI) where I started out as a student and later joined the faculty to become an instructor on business planning and the art of attracting capital. CEO Space is this country's top entrepreneurial forum where miracles happen on an hourly basis. I know because I've witnessed countless examples of them, including many in my life. It was at his business forum that my company The Mentor Network grew and thrived as we supported ever-increasing numbers of needy children around the world. It is also through the contacts I made at his forum that this book is being published. Thank you, Berny.

I wish to thank my two current business partners, Stephen Kent and Jim Woodhams, for their friendship and continued faith in me. It's been a great journey, and I know we have many places left to go.

Thank you also to those individuals who caused me hardship at times. It's because of you that I learned some of the lessons in this book.

Connect with Parviz

Facebook:

www.facebook.com/pfirouzgar

LinkedIn:

www.linkedin.com/pub/parviz-firouzgar/b6/8b4/91

Twitter:

@ParvizFirouzgar

Website:

www.ParvizFirouzgar.com

Email:

Parviz@ParvizFirouzgar.com

www.ingramcontent.com/pod-product-compliance
Lightning Source LLC
Chambersburg PA
CBHW060547200326
41521CB00007B/521